THE FAVOR FACTOR:

Discovering the missing ingredient
to a life of blessing and abundance

by David Cerullo

Copyright © 2014 by David Cerullo, Inspiration Ministries

ISBN: 9-781936-177240

Published by
INSPIRATION MINISTRIES
PO Box 7750
Charlotte, NC 28241
+1 803-578-1899

Printed in the United States of America.

All Scripture quotations, unless otherwise indicated, are from the *New King James Version* of the Bible, © 1982 by Thomas Nelson, Inc. Used by permission. All rights reserved.

> Scriptures marked **NASB** are from the *New American Standard Bible.*
> Scriptures marked **KJV** are from the *King James Version of the Bible.*
> Scriptures marked **NIV** are from the *New International Version of the Bible.*
> Scriptures marked **NLT** are from the *New Living Translation of the Bible.*
> Scriptures marked **ESV** are from the *English Standard Version of the Bible.*
> Scriptures marked **TLB** are from *The Living Bible paraphrase of the Bible.*
> Scriptures marked **MSG** are from *The Message paraphrase of the Bible.*

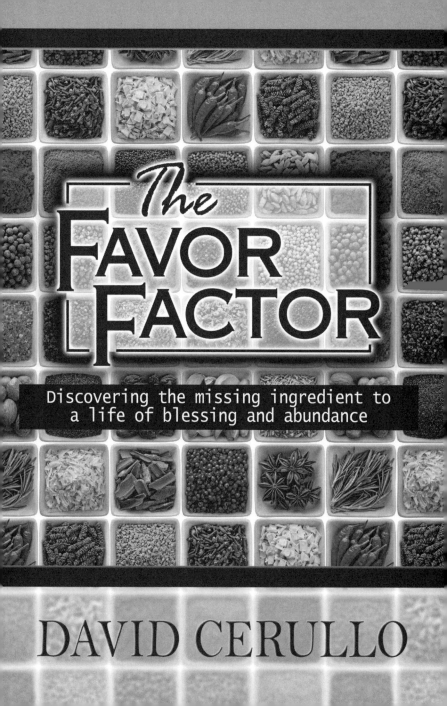

The FAVOR FACTOR

Discovering the missing ingredient to
a life of blessing and abundance

DAVID CERULLO

TABLE OF CONTENTS

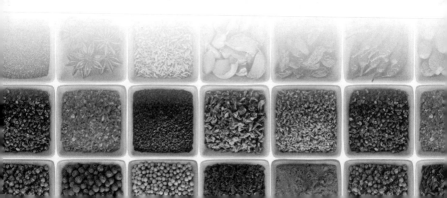

*"Let the favor of
the Lord our God be upon us,
and establish the work of our
hands upon us; yes,
establish the work of our hands!"*

– PSALM 90:17 NIV

Dear Friends,

From cover to cover, the Bible is a book about the favor of God. Its opening chapters describe the amazing favor given to our first ancestors, Adam and Eve. There was no poverty, sickness, or death in God's original creation. The first man and woman were placed in a beautiful garden, surrounded by lavish abundance...a testimony to the incredible favor of their loving Creator.

"God saw everything that He had made, and indeed it was very good" (Genesis 1:31). Your Heavenly Father never created you to suffer lack...experience disease...battle depression...or fight against your loved ones. No, His plan for you—right from the beginning—was one of blessing and favor:

> *"I know the plans I have for you,"* declares the Lord,
> *"plans to prosper you and not to harm you,*
> *plans to give you hope and a future"*
> (Jeremiah 29:11 NIV).

Have you discovered God's wonderful plans for your life, my friend? They are revealed throughout the Scriptures, and they will take hold in your life as you draw near to the Lord in prayer and worship.

Make a commitment today to pursue God's plan with all your heart. You'll be glad you did—both in this life and for all eternity.

God bless you!

David Cerullo

1 OPENING YOUR HEART TO GOD'S FAVOR

What exactly is the favor of God? How do you receive His favor? Is it possible to live in the favor of God every day? Can you be a child of God, a Christian, and NOT live in His favor?

Dictionaries describe favor as approval, support, kindness, esteem, and even unfair partiality. If I asked you, "Do you want God's approval? His support? His blessing? What about His kindness, esteem, and partiality?" I believe your answer would be, "YES!" Of course I do! We *all* do!

From cover to cover, the Bible teaches that *God loves you*, and He wants you to enjoy His favor as a beloved child. But the sad truth is that most people don't live in a place of God's favor. Even many Christians live their lives outside the favor of God, not really understanding what His favor is or how to receive it.

Understanding how the favor of God works is one of the most important lessons you can learn in life. But if you don't understand God's character, you won't understand His favor either.

God is not some cosmic being far out in the universe, disengaged from the cares and concerns of your life. He loves you. He cares about you. And He can be as close to you as the breath you breathe.

God wants to bless you and answer your prayers today. Jesus promised us, *"Ask, and it will be given to you; seek, and you will find;*

knock, and it will be opened to you" (Matthew 7:7). But then He went on to say that our confidence in petitioning God with our prayer requests is dependent on seeing Him as our loving Heavenly Father:

> *What man is there among you who, if his son asks for bread, will give him a stone? Or if he asks for a fish, will he give him a serpent? If you then, being evil, know how to give good gifts to your children, how much more will your Father who is in heaven give good things to those who ask Him!*
> (Matthew 7:9-11)

Let those words sink in for a moment. You have a Father in Heaven who wants to give you *"good things"* when you ask Him! As much as your earthly father may love you, your Heavenly Father loves you more… so much more. He longs to show you His kindness and approval…to bless you…and to give you good gifts.

You have a Father in Heaven who wants to give you "good things" when you ask Him!

You see, when you open your heart to God's wisdom and favor, *everything else* in your life is impacted. Not only will He re-energize your spiritual life, but there will be a transformation of your health, finances, emotions, and relationships as well. You can experience His supernatural favor—not just for a moment, but for a lifetime, and then for all eternity!

2 UNCONDITIONAL LOVE, CONDITIONAL PROMISES

Have you ever wondered, "If my Heavenly Father longs to give me good gifts…if He wants to bless me and show me His kindness and approval…why don't I seem to experience that on a regular basis?"

For a moment, picture in your mind God as your caring, loving Heavenly Father who wants to bless you with the good things of life. Then ask yourself, "Is it possible that His love and His blessings are two different things?"

I believe they are. His love is unconditional. There is nothing you can do to earn your Heavenly Father's love. He loves you… because He loves you…because He loves you. And there is nothing you can do to make Him stop loving you.

There is nothing you can do to earn your Heavenly Father's love.

But His approval, blessings, and favor are different from His love. Rather than being unconditional, they are conditional. And they *are* conditional on several different things.

For example, the Bible repeatedly emphasizes obedience as being one of the most important aspects of living in God's favor. Jesus described this on a number of different occasions:

Why do you call Me "Lord, Lord," and not do the things which I say? (Luke 6:46)

If you love Me, keep My commandments…He who has My commandments and keeps them, it is he who loves Me. And he who loves Me will be loved by My Father, and I will love him and manifest Myself to him (John 14:15, 14:21).

If you keep My commandments, you will abide in My love, just as I have kept My Father's commandments and abide in His love. These things I have spoken to you, that My joy may remain in you, and that your joy may be full (John 15:10-11).

One of the biggest things many Christians fail to realize is that the blessings and favor of God are not random occurrences of "good luck." His promises are clear, and they are 100% conditional. When you were in school and took math classes, you probably learned about things called "postulates." Postulates are "rules" you apply in math. Many of them can be summed up in phrases like, "IF this…THEN that."

You need to realize that there is always an "if" with God. He says over and over again, "If you'll do *this*…then I'll do that." Although His love remains unconditional, His favor requires obedience—meeting the conditions in His Word.

You and I are saved by God's grace. This favor is totally unmerited, for He demonstrated His love *"while we were still sinners"* (Romans 5:8). We didn't do anything to earn this unmerited favor. It's *"the gift of God, not of works, lest anyone should boast"* (Ephesians 2:8-9).

While we *earn* wages, gifts are different. A gift must be freely given, or else it isn't truly a gift.

When we receive God's amazing grace, we are receiving something wonderful that we didn't deserve. When we receive His mercy, He is withholding the punishment we *did* deserve.

You and I will never be saved by our works, but here's something interesting…we *will* be *rewarded* for our works. One day when we get to Heaven and stand before God, we'll be rewarded on the basis of our obedience and the works we did here on earth.

3 ATTRACTING GOD'S FAVOR

If I called you on the phone today and asked how I could pray for you, what would you say? Do you need God's healing touch? A financial breakthrough? The restoration of your marriage? Deliverance from an addiction? The salvation of your children or other loved ones?

Well, I have great news for you. There's only ONE thing you really need: God's favor! The psalmist understood this well, and he prayed, *"May the favor of the Lord our God rest on us; establish the work of our hands for us"* (Psalm 90:17 NIV). Do you want God to bless the work of your hands today? Then you need His favor above all else.

This comes from seeking the Lord with all our heart. When we do, everything else falls into place. That's why David could boldly say in Psalm 34:10, *"Those who seek the LORD lack no good thing."*

To David, this was more than a nice theory. He wrote about this in the 23rd Psalm. Because he had drawn near to the Lord as his Good Shepherd, he lacked nothing. And he was so confident of God's favor in his life that he proclaimed, *"Surely your goodness and love will follow me all the days of my life, and I will dwell in the house of the LORD forever."*

David knew all about this kind of favor. He had first experienced it years earlier when the prophet Samuel was seeking

God's direction on who Israel's next king should be (1 Samuel 16). Samuel knew the king was to be chosen from among the sons of Jesse, and so the sons were paraded before the prophet to see which one was the Lord's choice. Samuel must have been a little confused when none of the seven oldest sons met with God's approval, so he told Jesse: *"The LORD has not chosen these...Are these all the sons you have?"* (vs. 10-11 NIV)

Apparently, no one had thought to invite David! He was the youngest son, and he was out tending his father's sheep. You see, while everyone else was looking at factors like age and rank, God was looking for a man after His heart...someone who would fulfill His purposes.

So they sent for David and brought him in, and we read in verses 12 and 13:

The LORD said, "Rise and anoint him; this is the one." So Samuel took the horn of oil and anointed him in the presence of his brothers, and from that day on the Spirit of the LORD came powerfully upon David.

Friend, all the while, God was looking for a person He could show His favor to! Maybe you feel like you're just taking care of some smelly old sheep, forgotten somewhere behind all the "important" people. But remember that God is searching for people like David—who have their heart set on pleasing Him.

The Bible promises in 2 Chronicles 16:9 (NASB): *"The eyes of the LORD move to and fro throughout the earth that He may strongly support those whose heart is completely His."* I pray *you* are a candidate for this amazing favor and support from God today!

4 HONORING GOD

Honoring God is one of the most important keys to receiving His favor. What does it mean to honor God? Dictionaries define honor as "giving great respect." But what are the practical ways you can show honor and great respect to God?

One of the clearest ways you can show honor to the Lord is by doing what He asks! When you obey God's commandments and keep His statutes, you are honoring Him. But in contrast, you dishonor Him when you disobey Him.

I'm sure we all disobey God to some degree every day. We fall, we fail, and we come up short in our desire to please the Lord in our thoughts, words, and deeds.

Honoring God is a foundational step toward walking in His favor.

Yet the good news is that He is ready and willing to forgive us. All we have to do is ask. In His mercy, He will pick us up and set us on the right track again. So just because we fall, that's no reason not to get back up again.

Don't fall for the devil's lie that you've sinned so greatly that God cannot and will not forgive you. The blood of Jesus shed for you on the Cross is greater than every sin and shortcoming. There is *nothing* you or I can ever do to separate us from the love of God (Romans 8:38-39).

When you disobey His Word and do things you shouldn't do, you can humbly come back to Him. His arms will be wide open when you ask Him to forgive you and help you do better next time. It's that simple and that easy. God will welcome you with open arms.

It's not too late for the Lord to give you a fresh start as you learn to honor Him and put Him first in your life. So I encourage you today to trust Him. Obey Him. Keep His statutes and commandments. And as you do, He will be faithful to His Word and will bless you with His amazing grace and favor.

Remember: Honoring God is a foundational step toward walking in His favor. And His favor will change your life, my friend.

5 THE BLESSINGS OF ABRAHAM

One of God's great promises about His favor is found in Genesis 12:2: *"I will bless you…and you will be a blessing."* Stop for a moment, and think about what God is saying. Make this a personal promise to YOU: *"I will bless **YOU**…and **YOU** will be a blessing."*

Of course, some people will be quick to point out that God is speaking to *Abraham* when He makes this promise—not to us today. Well, that's partially true. God was talking to Abraham, but the Bible says the promises God made to Abraham, He also made to us:

> *Those who are of faith are sons of Abraham…Christ redeemed us from the curse of the law…that the blessing of Abraham might come upon the Gentiles in Christ Jesus, that we might receive the promise of the Spirit through faith… Now to Abraham and his Seed were the promises made* (Galatians 3:7-14).

You see, the covenant promises made to Abraham are promises made to YOU as a spiritual descendant of Abraham. God made a binding agreement with Abraham and his descendants to BLESS them—and you and I have inherited those covenant blessings!

God is a covenant-making God. He wanted a *relationship* with Abraham and with those who would follow in his footsteps of faith, and that's what this covenant is all about.

When Barbara and I got married, we exchanged vows. We made promises to each other to love and cherish one another for the rest of our lives. Our love relationship was sealed by the covenant we made with each other before God and all our wedding guests. This is the kind of love relationship the Lord wants to have with you. He loves you so much that He wants you to live in a covenant relationship with Him *forever*.

A covenant is a solemn, binding agreement between two parties. To covenant with someone means that those involved will stand behind their word, no matter what. Just as Barbara and I made a covenant promise to be faithful to one another as husband and wife until the day we die, God has made covenant promises to you—promises that extend all the way into eternity.

God won't forget His covenant promises, my friend. He will stand behind His Word every time, and He will *never* be unfaithful to what He has covenanted with you to do. He will never lie, as we are told in Numbers 23:19: *"God is not a man, that He should lie, nor a son of man, that He should repent; has He said, and will He not do it? Or has He spoken, and will He not make it good?"*

Remember: Faithfulness is God's part of the covenant, and your part is to trust and obey. When you honor Him with your faith and obedience, you can boldly claim the countless promises in His Word.

6 THE FAVOR FORMULA

As we've already seen, receiving God's favor is not a matter of chance or happenstance. His favor is released when we meet the conditions in His Word. Although each of the promises in the Bible has its own set of conditions, there is a general "Favor Formula" that applies in every situation:

HONORING GOD + FAITH + OBEDIENCE + EXPECTANCY = GOD'S FAVOR, BLESSINGS, AND APPROVAL

I've already touched on what it means to **honor God**, and *faith* is another crucial ingredient in a life that enjoys God's favor. The Lord says in Hebrews 11:6 that without faith, it is *impossible* to please Him. By faith, men and women throughout the Scriptures believed God's promises and trusted Him to intervene in their circumstances.

Faith means trusting God, *"who gives life to the dead and calls those things which do not exist as though they did"* (Romans 4:17). It means being confident He will intervene in your circumstances. And it gives us assurance that *"God causes all things to work together for good to those who love God, to those who are called according to His purpose"* (Romans 8:28 NASB).

Obedience means putting your faith into action, which happens when you read God's Word, follow what it says, and obey the voice of the Holy Spirit. Jesus tells us in John 15:14, *"You are*

*My friends if you **do** whatever I command you."*

My friend Dr. Charles Stanley said to me one day, "David, learn to obey God and leave the consequences to Him." I'll never forget that. It's not always easy to obey what we believe God is telling us to do, but it's a crucial part of living in His favor.

You can trust that God is who He says He is and that He will do what He says He will do.

Expectancy is another key that opens the door to God's favor. Expectancy is hope-filled waiting that only comes after you've prayed in faith, believed God will intervene in your circumstances, and been obedient to His Word and His Holy Spirit. It's crucial to wrap your faith and obedience with expectation, trusting God and expecting Him to be faithful to His covenant promises.

You can trust that God is who He says He is and that He will *do* what He says He will do. He promises in Jeremiah 1:12 that He will watch over His Word to perform it.

So if you're seeking more of God's favor in your finances, health, relationships, or peace of mind, I encourage you to follow the example of Bible heroes who received breakthroughs when they applied the formula of **HONORING GOD + FAITH + OBEDIENCE + EXPECTANCY**. You will receive God's favor, blessings, and approval, and He will intervene in your difficult circumstances in amazing ways.

7 KINGDOM PRIORITIES

David wrote in Psalm 5:12, *"Surely, Lord, you bless the righteous; you surround them with your favor as with a shield."* Isn't that a beautiful observation? God's favor can encircle you like a shield, protecting you on all sides. It can shield you against any pressures the enemy tries to use to keep you from receiving all the blessings God has for you.

The Bible describes the devil as a thief who comes *"to steal and kill and destroy"* (John 10:10 NIV). However, the shield of God's favor will come between you and the forces of evil that seek to destroy you...forces too powerful and cunning for you to deal with in your own strength or wisdom. You have no protection against these forces except the invisible, but also *invincible*, shield of the Lord's favor in your life.

But remember: Who does God surround with His favor as with a shield? *"The righteous."* This ties in with Jesus' instruction in Matthew 6:33 to *"seek first the kingdom of God and His righteousness, and all these things shall be added to you."* When you truly put God's Kingdom and His righteousness first in your life, you can be confident of His favor—and

> *When you truly put God's Kingdom and His righteousness first in your life, you can be confident of His favor.*

that favor will protect us as a shield.

Friend, examine your priorities today. Are you seeking first God's Kingdom and His righteousness? Are you praying, as Jesus taught in Matthew 6:10, for His Kingdom to come and His will to be done in your life? As you align your priorities with God's priorities, you will ensure the protection and security that come from living in His favor.

Make sure you are looking in the *right place* for your security and peace. People may let you down. Political and financial institutions may crumble. But there is one thing in life that you can count on: God surrounds the righteous with favor.

8 INCREASING IN FAVOR

I'm always surprised that so many Christians seem unaware of the importance of God's favor. Many are also ignorant of the Biblical principles God lays out for *receiving* and *growing* in His favor.

Here at Inspiration Ministries, we receive prayer requests from many people who are looking for a breakthrough or a promotion of some kind. Some are looking for a new job, or maybe they are hoping their boss will recognize their value and give them a raise.

When you increase in God's wisdom, you will also grow in your ability to receive His favor.

Over the years, we've discovered that a vital key to a breakthrough like that is receiving the favor of God. Luke 2:52 tells us, *"Jesus increased in wisdom and stature, and in favor with God and men."* There are several vital points to see here. First, this verse teaches that when you increase in God's *wisdom,* you will also grow in your ability to receive His favor. So it's critical that you seek God's wisdom, and that comes primarily as you study His Word and spend time in His presence.

Second, Luke 2:52 lets us know that we can increase in the favor of God. You're not just stuck with some level of favor that you've inherited from your parents or received because of what you've done or not done in the past. God can propel you to new levels of His supernatural favor *today!*

The third principle we see in Luke 2:52 is that there's a connection between *God's* favor and the favor we are seeking from a boss, a potential employer, or even a loved one or potential mate. Jesus increased in favor *"with God AND men"*—not just God alone. Do you see what good news this is? As your ways are pleasing to the Lord, He not only gives you HIS favor, but He also causes PEOPLE to give you favor for the things you need in life.

I love what the psalmist writes in Psalm 75:6-7: *"Exaltation comes neither from the east nor from the west nor from the south. But God is the Judge: He puts down one, and exalts another."* My friend, this means you need to look to GOD for your promotion and advancement. Yes, He will use people to carry out His will and extend His favor, but make no mistake about it: Your promotion must ultimately come from HIM.

And what is it that triggers this kind of promotion from the Lord? James 4:6-10 cites humility as the key ingredient: *"God resists the proud, but gives grace to the humble. Therefore submit to God. Resist the devil and he will flee from you. Draw near to God and He will draw near to you. Humble yourselves in the sight of the Lord, and He will lift you up."*

God has made the pathway to His favor very clear. I encourage you to humble yourself before Him today. Wholeheartedly give Him your life, and watch Him pour out His abundant blessings and favor!

9 REGAINING GOD'S FAVOR

We've discussed *receiving* the favor of God, and also how to increase in that favor. However, what can we do when we've forfeited the Lord's favor through sin and disobedience? What steps can we take in order to restore the favor we've lost?

Thankfully, in 2 Chronicles 7:14 God gives us some powerful principles for restoration. Although this verse is often used as a prescription for unlocking God's favor upon a nation, the principles also apply to individuals like you and me:

> *If My people who are called by My name will humble themselves, and pray and seek My face, and turn from their wicked ways, then I will hear from heaven, and will forgive their sin and heal their land.*

God's prescription here is very clear. First of all, He says this formula is only meant to apply to *His people*. We certainly can't hope to receive the full measure of the Lord's favor if we haven't truly given our life to Him.

Second, God wants us to see the power that comes in being *called by His name*. When we're walking in a covenant relationship with God, we can use the mighty name of Jesus in

The Lord wants to heal everything in your life today, including your health, emotions, finances, and relationships.

our prayers and in our battles against the forces of darkness.

The next thing God says in 2 Chronicles 7:14 is that we must *humble ourselves* if we are going to receive our breakthrough of favor. And as we humble ourselves, we must also *pray, seek God's face,* and *turn from any wicked ways.* As you spend quality time in the Lord's presence each day, make sure to ask Him to reveal any *"wicked ways"*—things that displease Him and hinder His favor in your life.

When you follow God's instructions in 2 Chronicles 7:14, He promises *to forgive your sins* and *heal your land.* But I believe the scope of this promise is very broad: The Lord wants to heal EVERYTHING in your life today, including your health, emotions, finances, and relationships.

Make it your goal today to please God in everything you do. Humble yourself before Him. Cry out to Him, and trust Him to pour out His supernatural favor and blessings in your life.

10 CHILDLIKE HUMILITY AND FAITH

In Matthew 18:2-4, Jesus describes the need for radical humility and faith in a rather unusual context:

Jesus called a little child to him and put the child among them. Then he said, "I tell you the truth, unless you turn from your sins and become like little children, you will never get into the Kingdom of Heaven. So anyone who becomes as humble as this little child is the greatest in the Kingdom of Heaven."

Perhaps you've never thought of young children as being particularly "humble," but let's explore what Jesus meant by this. First of all, little children are *teachable*. If you are going to receive the full measure of God's favor in your life, it's crucial to allow Him to teach you the principles in His Word for tapping into the abundant resources of Heaven.

If you are going to receive the full measure of God's favor in your life, it's crucial to allow Him to teach you the principles in His Word.

Another characteristic of young children is that they typically find it very easy to trust their parents. If their mom or dad tells them something, they haven't yet learned to question it. This is important in the context of God's favor as well. Our Heavenly Father has given us countless promises in His Word, but those promises must be activated by *faith*. Only as we trust God and put our faith in His promises will we receive the benefit of those promises.

Finally, while teenagers often go through a time of rebellion against their parents' authority, very young children usually find it much easier to *obey* their parents' commands. Again, this is a pivotal issue in our quest to receive God's favor in our lives. His promises are conditional, not just on our faith, but also on our obedience.

Do you see why Jesus says we must have child-like faith, obedience, and teachableness in order to be great in His Kingdom? Jesus taught us in Matthew 6:33 that when we seek first His Kingdom and His righteousness, He will give us *everything else* we need! But our pursuit of God's Kingdom blessings must be with the child-like traits I've described.

This takes real humility. We all want to think we are smart enough and capable enough to handle things on our own, but humility means recognizing our need for *God's* wisdom and favor—just as a little child recognizes his dependence on His parents.

Take a moment to pause and reflect on these vital attributes of living in God's favor. Humble yourself before Him, and acknowledge your need for His wisdom and strength.

11 The Power of Forgiveness

Forgiveness is an indispensable component for releasing God's favor in your life. There are two sides of this powerful force: First, you must receive God's forgiveness for the sins you've committed, and then you must also forgive anyone you feel has sinned against you.

The Bible teaches that we all fall short of God's perfect standard (Romans 3:23). Nevertheless, because of His great love, He is ready and willing to forgive us. As 1 John 1:9 tells us, all we have to do is ask for God's forgiveness and cleansing: *"If we confess our sins, He is faithful and just to forgive us our sins and to cleanse us from all unrighteousness."*

There is NO condemnation when you are positioned in Christ – not even a smidgen!

Isn't that great news? When we acknowledge our sins and come before the Lord, He is faithful to forgive us and cleanse us. Isaiah 1:18 says, *"Though your sins are like scarlet, they shall be as white as snow; though they are red like crimson, they shall be as wool."*

Once we receive God's forgiveness, it's crucial that we not continue to wallow in defeat or condemnation. We must pick ourselves up and get going again. Even if we've fallen repeatedly, that's no reason not to get back up again.

We're told in Proverbs 24:16 (NIV): *"Though the righteous fall seven times, they rise again, but the wicked stumble when calamity strikes."* So if you've failed in some way today, you can rise again! How? David explains in Psalm 37:23-24: *"The steps of a good man are ordered by the LORD, and He delights in his way. Though he fall, he shall not be utterly cast down; for the LORD upholds him with His hand."*

Let these encouraging words sink in for a moment. Even though you may fall at times, you need to remember that God delights in you. In your darkest hour, remember that He will *uphold you* with His mighty hand.

When we disobey God's Word and do things we shouldn't have done, His arms will be wide open to us nevertheless. Like the prodigal son in Luke 15, we simply must get up from our pigpen and return home. We must ask the Lord to forgive us and help us do better next time. It's that simple and that easy. God will always welcome us with open arms.

I encourage you to meditate on these great words from the apostle Paul in Romans 8:1: *"There is therefore now **no condemnation** to those who are in Christ Jesus."* Declare this beautiful verse over and over again until it sinks deeply into your heart.

There is **NO** condemnation when you are positioned in Christ—not even a smidgen! You are totally forgiven and accepted by your Heavenly Father—ready to receive His amazing favor in every area of your life.

12 RELEASING FAVOR THROUGH GENEROSITY

Over many years of walking with the Lord, my wife Barbara and I have repeatedly seen God's faithfulness in releasing His favor when we practice generosity. Even when it seems like everything else has failed to bring us the breakthrough we need, generosity often has unlocked God's favor and abundance in amazing ways.

Barbara and I have discovered, again and again, that you truly cannot out-give God. Those who live lives of radical generosity consistently experience an overflow of God's blessings in their lives.

So are you ready to be blessed like you've never been blessed before? Generosity may well be a key you've overlooked.

Solomon tells us in Proverbs 11:25, *"A generous person will prosper; whoever refreshes others will be refreshed."* This is such a clear and powerful statement by the wisest man who ever lived. If we want to prosper, we must learn to live a life of generosity toward God's Kingdom and the needs of others.

Let's be honest: Generosity doesn't always come easily. But the first step is to recognize that *everything* we have is a gift from God. This means that we are merely stewards—trustees or managers—of the time, talent, and treasure we have received from the Lord.

The great men and women of faith described in the Bible all understood this critical truth. For example, David writes in 1 Chronicles 29:10-13 (NIV):

Praise be to you, LORD, the God of our father Israel, from everlasting to everlasting. Yours, LORD, is the greatness and the power and the glory and the majesty and the splendor, for EVERYTHING in heaven and earth is yours. Yours, LORD, is the kingdom; you are exalted as head over all. Wealth and honor come from you; you are the ruler of all things. In your hands are strength and power to exalt and give strength to all. Now, our God, we give you thanks, and praise your glorious name.

Do you see how this perspective will change your life? It's not so hard to give if you recognize that it's not really yours in the first place. Also, realize that just as God has given you everything you already hold in your hands, you can receive even GREATER abundance when you faithfully give of what to have—regularly sowing seeds into God's Kingdom and the lives of others.

Jesus describes this principle in Luke 6:38 when He says, *"Give, and it will be given to you. A good measure, pressed down, shaken together and running over, will be poured into your lap. For with the measure you use, it will be measured to you."*

What a beautiful picture of the kind of overflowing abundance and favor our Heavenly Father wants to give to His children. But it all starts with that important word: *"GIVE…"* So remember: Favor is released from God's hands when we release something He has given us from OUR hands.

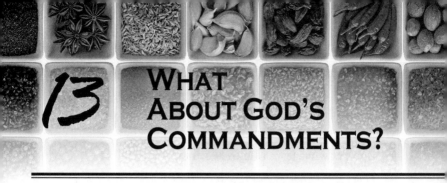

13 WHAT ABOUT GOD'S COMMANDMENTS?

God's favor is a powerful force, with the ability to totally transform your finances, health, relationships, peace of mind—and every other area of your life as well. So it would be a very valuable discovery to figure out what ingredients you need to unleash that force in your life.

The good news is that the ingredients for a life of favor don't have to be a mystery. You don't have to be like a mad scientist, frantically mixing random chemicals in search of a concoction that will release the favor of God in your life. No, the ingredients you need for God's favor have been clearly described for you throughout His Word.

Sadly, though, it has become fashionable to dismiss many vital ingredients as unnecessary or unimportant. Many Christians have misinterpreted salvation by grace to mean they can enjoy the favor of God without adhering to His commandments.

God gave His people 10 Commandments, not 10 suggestions (see Exodus 20:1-17). Christians and Jews alike call these "the Law." They are not God's *entire* law, of course, but they form the foundation for the rest of the law. In fact, the 10 Commandments form the foundation not only for God's spiritual law, but they've also been adopted as the foundation for our civil code of law in the United States and many other nations.

Many Christians assume that since we now live under grace,

the Law doesn't apply to us any longer. That is partially correct, for the Law was never intended to be the means of our salvation. However, to say that God's moral law doesn't apply to us any longer is to misunderstand what the Bible teaches.

Look at what Jesus said in Matthew 5:17-19:

Don't think that I came to abolish the Law or the Prophets;
I did not come to abolish but to fulfill. For truly I say to you,
until heaven and earth pass away, not the smallest letter
or stroke shall pass from the Law until all is accomplished.
Whoever then annuls one of the least of these commandments,
and teaches others to do the same, shall be called least in the
kingdom of heaven; but whoever keeps and teaches them, he
shall be called great in the kingdom of heaven.

How does this apply to other passages of Scripture, such as Romans 3:28, which teach that we are saved by the grace of God and not by our keeping of the Law? The principles found in God's moral law still apply today if we want to live a life pleasing to Him, filled with His favor. Obviously, He isn't pleased when someone murders, steals, or commits adultery. Grace doesn't change any of that. Yes, we can be forgiven, justified by faith (Romans 5:1), but the principles in the Law describe the things that please the Lord—and the things that don't.

This should be our aim in everything we do, as Paul told the Corinthians: *"We make it our goal to please him"* (2 Corinthians 5:9 NIV). Before we go any further in our study, take a moment to pause and ask the Lord to examine your heart. Are you devoted to a life of pleasing Him? This is an important part of experiencing His favor and releasing His blessings.

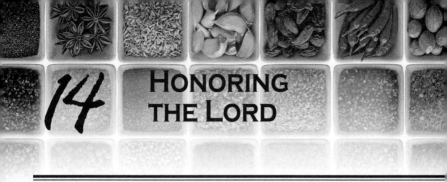

14 HONORING THE LORD

One of the 10 Commandments tells us: *"Honor your father and your mother, that your days may be prolonged in the land which the LORD your God gives you"* (Exodus 20:12). This verse plainly says that if you honor your father and mother, you will live a long and blessed life. The converse is also true: If you dishonor your father and mother, God's favor will be undermined, and your life will be shortened.

If God put so much importance on honoring our earthly father and mother, just think how important it also is that we honor HIM as our Heavenly Father. In fact, honor is a powerful catalyst for God's favor in our lives. So what does it mean to truly honor the Lord?

Dictionaries define honor as "giving great respect," and there are 134 verses in the Bible that talk about honor. It's clearly an important topic to God, and many of the promises in His Word are directly related to our willingness to honor Him. Honor is another example of God's *"IF you do this…THEN I'll do that"* postulates.

Honor will lead you to favor, and favor will open wide the gateway to God's blessings in your life.

You show honor to the Lord by obeying His commandments and doing what He asks. But you dishonor Him if you disobey

Him. It's that simple.

If you honor the Lord, He will honor you. Honor will lead you to favor, and favor will open wide the gateway to His blessings in your life.

Do you want to release more of God's honor and favor in your life? Then the Bible's instruction is clear: *"Pride brings a person low, but the lowly in spirit gain honor"* (Proverbs 29:23 NIV). Whenever we truly humble ourselves before the Lord, He has promised to lift us up (1 Peter 5:6).

The Bible also teaches that we can honor God by bringing Him the *"firstfruits"* of our income: *"Honor the LORD with your possessions, and with the firstfruits of all your increase; so your barns will be filled with plenty, and your vats will overflow with new wine"* (Proverbs 3:9-10).

This is one of the most important verses in the Bible describing how to be blessed by God and receive His favor. The *"firstfruits"* principle means that when you get a paycheck, the first 10% belongs to the Lord, not just what's left over (*if* anything is left over). If you want to receive the full measure of His blessings, make sure to honor Him—and this begins with giving Him the first 10% of all you earn.

15 FAILURE DOESN'T HAVE TO BE FINAL

Failure is something we've all experienced at one time or another. Sometimes the failure is pretty insignificant: a poor grade on a test…striking out on our little league baseball team… flunking our first driving test when we're a teen. But other failures are a lot more painful: a lost job…a divorce…rebellious children…financial ruin.

The Bible is very candid about the failures of its heroes. Although some of the failures seemed fairly minor, at other times God's grace brought a hero from complete devastation into a new beginning of success and victory.

The apostle Peter experienced extreme failure before God brought him to a place of extreme fruitfulness. One of the remarkable things about Peter's story is that Jesus clearly knew all about Peter's weaknesses—yet He chose him anyway.

Let me encourage you today: God knows all about your weaknesses and failures too, but His grace is able to restore you and give you the new beginning you need. He will take you from failure to favor.

Peter was just a fisherman by trade. He wasn't the kind of guy you would think of when looking for someone to be the spiritual leader of thousands of people. Yet Jesus didn't see Peter as we might have seen him: a crude, smelly, uneducated tradesman. Somehow Jesus saw Peter as a person of great promise and destiny.

We might have questioned Jesus' judgment in choosing such a person, asking Him, "Jesus, why would You pick someone who is so 'earthy'…so poor…so uneducated…so prone to arguments…so spiritually untrained?"

God knows all about your weaknesses and failures, but His grace is able to restore you and give you the new beginning you need.

But Jesus knew that Peter's real obstacle was something completely different than any of these outward factors: *He was full of pride and self-reliance.*

This character flaw is no minor issue! It goes to the very heart of whether or not we are truly usable by God. King Solomon—who seems to have had his own struggles with pride and self-reliance—warns us, *"Trust in the LORD with all your heart, and lean not on your own understanding"* (Proverbs 3:5). This is a difficult lesson for any of us to learn, and it was particularly hard for self-reliant Peter.

Although Peter always stood out among the other disciples, it wasn't always for the best of reasons. Sometimes he stood out because he was the "star pupil"—the one who had the right answer to Jesus' probing questions. However, at other times he stood out because he became a dunce—someone prone to stick his foot in his mouth.

And in Peter's case, there often was a rather quick transition between speaking what the Spirit of God had revealed to him and then, only moments later, blurting out something inspired by the devil. Matthew 16:13-19 gives the wonderful account of Peter's revelation of Jesus' true identity. When the disciples were asked by Jesus, *"Who do you say that I am?"* Peter was ready with a quick, accurate answer: *"You are the Christ, the Son of the living God!"*

Good answer, Peter! Jesus was so excited that He told Peter the entire church would be built upon this revelation. Those who see Jesus as He is will also be given *"the keys of the Kingdom"* (vs. 18-19). Peter was undoubtedly feeling pretty impressed with himself at this point.

But the chapter doesn't end there. Peter, who had just been applauded by the Lord, was about to say something stupid and get a major rebuke when he tried to persuade Jesus from going to the Cross (v. 22). Peter undoubtedly meant well, and he must have been shocked by Jesus response: *"Get behind Me, Satan! You are an offense to Me, for you are not mindful of the things of God, but the things of men"* (v. 23).

Because of his pride and self-reliance, Jesus' star pupil had unwittingly put himself in league with Satan! It seems to have taken Peter mere minutes to go from the mountain top to the valley. Have you ever had a failure like that—right after feeling you were on the top of the world?

Peter later failed an even bigger test when Jesus was arrested, and Peter denied even knowing the Lord. Yet Jesus knows all about every sin we've ever committed or ever will commit—and He loves us anyway. In Peter's case, Jesus not only predicted his failure, but He also predicted his restoration (Luke 22:31-32).

Isn't this a wonderful story? Jesus can see past our failures to a day when we will be restored and re-commissioned for fruitful service. He knows we will experience failure at times but, as in Peter's case, He is predicting our *ultimate victory.*

Friend, your failures don't have to be final. This can be your new day of God's forgiveness and favor.

16 TRUSTING A FAITHFUL GOD

The prophet Jeremiah faced some dark days, especially when his beloved city of Jerusalem was ransacked by an invading army. Nevertheless, when things seemed darkest, He saw the reassuring light of God's love and favor break through in a powerful way:

What God has promised you, He will do. Trust Him!

The LORD'S loving kindnesses indeed never cease, for His compassions never fail. They are new every morning; great is Your faithfulness. "The LORD is my portion," says my soul, "Therefore I have hope in Him." The LORD is good to those who wait for Him, to the person who seeks Him. It is good that he waits silently for the salvation of the LORD (Lamentations 3:22–26 NASB).

Take a few moments to meditate on the wonderful words and concepts in this passage: the Lord's loving kindnesses… compassions…faithfulness…provision…hope…salvation. Although he found himself in difficult circumstances, Jeremiah proclaimed that *"the LORD is good."* Make that your proclamation as well today. No matter how dark your situation may seem, declare God's goodness and faithfulness. *He is good all the time!*

But notice that Jeremiah also recognized his need to *"wait"* for the Lord to fulfill His Word. The Hebrew word for *"wait"* is *qavah*, which means to wait with hope and expectancy. This is not glum or passive waiting, but rather faith-filled anticipation that God will be faithful to carry out the promises of His word.

Remember, my friend: You can always trust that God is who He says He is, and that He will do what He says He will do. Perhaps Jeremiah had been tempted to doubt this, but the Lord told him plainly: *"I am watching over my word to perform it"* (Jeremiah 1:12 NASB).

That is His message to you today as well. What God has promised you, He will do. *Trust Him!*

17 EXPECTING MIRACLES

The Bible is filled with inspiring stories of people who approached the Lord in faith, desperate for some kind of breakthrough. Jairus was one of the rulers of the synagogue, and his little daughter was lying sick, at the point of death (Mark 5:22-42). Yet he recognized that Jesus could heal her and raise her up: *"Come and lay Your hands on her, that she may be healed, and she will live"* (v. 23).

Notice that there was no uncertainty in Jairus' request. He knew he needed a miracle, but he was absolutely convinced Jesus was willing and able to provide it.

What request do you have of the Lord today? Healing for yourself or a loved one? A financial breakthrough? The lifting of fear or depression? A restored relationship? A better job? Make sure your request is clear and specific.

Next, make sure you have truly asked God for the miracle you need. This may seem obvious, but sometimes we fret and complain about a situation, while never truly presenting it to the Lord and asking for His help. James 4:2 says, *"You do not have because you do not ask."*

As you make your request to God, remember to add **FAITH + OBEDIENCE + EXPECTANCY,** just as Jairus did when he wanted Jesus to heal his daughter. The Bible doesn't just say that anything is possible, it says, *"All things are possible to him* *who BELIEVES"* (Mark 9:27).

Finally, don't be surprised if your faith is tested before the breakthrough comes. While Jesus was still on His way to the bedside of Jairus' daughter, news came that the girl had already died. There seemed to be no further point in Jesus' coming to pray for her healing.

But Jesus made a powerful statement about FAITH must overcome FEAR in our life: *"Do not be afraid; only believe"* (v. 36). After having the doubters leave the girl's room, He took her by the hand and raised her from the dead. People were *"overcome with great amazement"* (v. 42), but this outcome is what Jairus had expected all along.

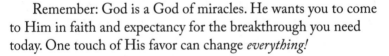

One touch of the Lord's favor can change everything!

Remember: God is a God of miracles. He wants you to come to Him in faith and expectancy for the breakthrough you need today. One touch of His favor can change *everything!*

18 HE WILL LIFT YOU UP

When thinking about the keys to receiving God's favor, people often overlook the importance of humility. Famed New England preacher Jonathan Edwards once observed, "Nothing sets a person so much out of the devil's reach as humility." So true.

Luke 9:46-48 tells about a time when Jesus' disciples were arguing with each other about which one of them was His greatest follower. These men clearly had the wrong idea about what it means to be great in God's Kingdom, and the Bible says the Lord challenged them about this: *"Jesus, knowing their thoughts, took a little child and had him stand beside him. Then he said to them, "Whoever welcomes this little child in my name welcomes me; and whoever welcomes me welcomes the one who sent me. For it is the one who is least among you all who is the greatest."*

One of the most powerful keys to unlocking God's blessings is to humble yourself and learn to serve Him and other people.

You see, the path to God's favor does not lie in exalting yourself and trying to get ahead of others. To the contrary, true greatness means humbling yourself before God and learning to be a servant.

Jesus described this contrast again in Mark 10:42-45, when He told the disciples, *"You know that those who are regarded as rulers of the Gentiles lord it over them, and their high officials exercise authority over them. Not so with you. Instead, whoever wants to become great among you must be your servant, and whoever wants to be first must be slave of all. For even the Son of Man did not come to be served, but to serve, and to give his life as a ransom for many."*

Jesus not only prescribed humility and servant-hood for His disciples, but He modeled these qualities in His own life, as the apostle Paul noted:

*Let this mind be in you which was also in Christ Jesus, who, being in the form of God, did not consider it robbery to be equal with God, but made Himself of **no reputation,** taking the form of a **bond-servant**, and coming in the likeness of men. And being found in appearance as a man, He **humbled Himself** and became obedient to the point of death, even the death of the cross.*

***Therefore God also has highly exalted Him** and given Him the name which is above every name, that at the name of Jesus every knee should bow…and that every tongue should confess that Jesus Christ is Lord, to the glory of God the Father* (Philippians 2:5-11).

What a stunning example of the pathway to God's favor. Jesus voluntarily emptied Himself and became of *"no reputation."* Though He was the Lord of Glory, He willingly took on *"the form of a bond-servant,"* humbling Himself and being obedient to the point of death.

So what was the result of Jesus' amazing humility, servant-hood, and obedience? Paul says, *"THEREFORE God also has highly exalted Him…"* What a great example for us! Because Jesus humbled Himself and obeyed the Father, He was highly exalted. As He laid down His life to do His Father's will, He received great favor and authority.

Friend, the Bible says you have a Heavenly Father who loves you and wants to bless you abundantly. But it's crucial to understand the keys you need to *unlock* those blessings.

Today you may be looking for a promotion at work…the lifting of depression…a restored relationship…or a financial breakthrough. Then remember: One of the most powerful keys to unlocking God's blessings is to humble yourself and learn to serve Him and other people. When you do, He has promised to give you His favor and lift you UP!

CHASED BY GOD'S BLESSINGS

19

Deuteronomy 28:1-14 paints a beautiful picture of some of the blessings you can expect when you are walking the favor of God. Not only does God say you will *receive* these blessings if you obey Him, but He says they will *"overtake you"* (v. 2). In other words, instead of you having to chase God's blessings, they will chase YOU!

And notice how all-inclusive God's blessings will be when you have His favor:

- In every place you go, whether in the city and in the country (v. 3).
- In the health of your body and the fruit of your labor (v. 4).
- In both your coming in and your going out (v. 6).
- In gaining victory over your enemies (v. 7).
- In being blessed in EVERYTHING you set your hand to (v. 8).
- In being established as a *"holy people"* to the Lord (v. 9).
- In experiencing a life of plenty, with God opening *"His good treasure"* to you (v. 11).
- In becoming *"the head and not the tail"* (v. 13).

But notice, once again, that there are *conditions* attached to this abundant favor. All of the blessings listed in Deuteronomy 28 are based on our response to God's invitation in verse 1: *"Now it shall come to pass, IF you diligently obey the voice of the LORD your God, to observe carefully all His commandments which I command you today…"*

Too often, when we read God's promises in Scripture, we overlook the conditions He includes in the context. If we expect to experience the kind of favor described in Deuteronomy 28, we must obey His voice and observe His commandments!

Take a few moments to pause and allow the Lord to speak to you. If there some teaching in His Word that you've been ignoring? Have you hardened your heart to the voice of His Spirit in some way?

Make a fresh commitment to live a life that is pleasing to the Lord. Then get ready for a tidal wave of His blessings to overtake you!

20 PRESSING THROUGH THE CROWD

When Jesus died for our sins on the Cross, the huge veil in the temple was torn in two, from top to bottom (Mark 15:38). This signified that God had opened the doorway into His presence, once and for all. Prior to that, only the high priest could enter the Holy of Holies, and even he could only approach God like that once a year.

But although God has graciously made a way for us to enter His presence and receive His blessings, we see another principle at work in the story of a woman who had suffered for 12 years with *"constant bleeding"* (Mark 5:24-34 NLT). Not only had she suffered from her health issues, but we're also told, *"She had suffered a great deal from many doctors, and over the years she had spent everything she had to pay them, but she had gotten no better. In fact, she had gotten worse"* (v. 26).

This woman's turning point came when she heard about Jesus one day. Faith and expectancy rose in her heart as she said to herself, *"If I can just touch his robe, I will be healed"* (v. 28).

Yet this woman had to overcome a serious obstacle in her pathway to a miracle. A large crowd of people thronged around Jesus as He walked

It's time to stir your faith, press through the obstacles, and reach out to touch the Lord for your breakthrough.

the dusty streets, making it extremely difficult for her to reach Him and touch His robe.

Perhaps this is how *you* are feeling today, my friend. You are desperate for a miracle in some area of your life, but many things seem to be obstructing your access to Jesus. Are you willing to do what this woman did, pressing through the crowd of obstacles until she could reach out and touch the Lord?

When the woman touched Jesus' robe, her bleeding immediately stopped. Twelve years of suffering were gone after one brief touch of the favor of God.

But notice that not everyone in the massive crowd received a miracle that day. Many were close enough to touch Jesus, but only this woman touched Him with the *faith and expectancy* needed to receive her healing. As a result, Jesus realized that *"healing power had gone out from him"* (v. 30).

When He discovered who it was who had touched Him with such faith, Jesus said to the woman, *"Daughter, your faith has made you well. Go in peace. Your suffering is over"* (v. 34).

Is there some issue in your life that you've suffered with for a long time? Then it's time to stir your faith, press through the obstacles, and reach out to touch the Lord for your breakthrough.

Remember: Jesus has already done the hard part for you on the Cross, ripping open the gateway to Heaven's abundant blessings. But you still may need to press through some difficult things that have obstructed you from receiving His favor in the past. Don't give up. Today can be a day of new beginnings for you!

21 ABUNDANCE FOR EVERY GOOD WORK

Often I meet people who act as if God's financial favor is a complete mystery to them. Yet the Word of God is full of principles for us to follow in order to release His prosperity in our lives.

One of the Lord's clear conditions for a life of financial blessing is to be faithful in sowing our tithes and offerings into His Kingdom. Although there are many other Biblical principles for unleashing God's financial favor, this is an indispensable starting point we can't afford to neglect.

One of the Lord's clear conditions for a life of financial blessing is to be faithful in sowing our tithes and offerings into His Kingdom.

Paul spends 2 Corinthians 9 on this important subject of financial stewardship:

> *He who sows sparingly will also reap sparingly, and he who sows bountifully will also reap bountifully. So let each one give as he purposes in his heart, not grudgingly or of necessity; for God loves a cheerful giver* (vs. 6-7).

To paraphrase Paul's words here, if you don't like what you are reaping, then you need to change what you are sowing. You can't expect to reap an abundant harvest if you are sowing miserly seeds. And Paul adds that we should also do an "attitude check" when we sow into God's Kingdom, making sure that we are giving cheerfully rather than grudgingly.

Many people have the terrible misconception that they shouldn't expect anything when they sow their financial seeds. What a tragic error! Can you imagine any farmer who would plant seeds in the ground without any expectation of an eventual harvest?

Immediately after telling the Corinthians to sow bountiful-ly in the Kingdom, Paul provides this beautiful promise about the harvest they will receive for their faithfulness: *"God is able to make all grace abound toward you, that you, always having all suf-ficiency in all things, may have an abundance for every good work"* (2 Corinthians 9:8).

Take a moment to let these words sink in. Wouldn't you like to have *"all sufficiency in all things"*? Wouldn't it be wonderful to have *"an abundance for every good work"*?

You may want to take a look at some other translations to see how fantastic Paul's statement is here. For example, the NLT says it this way: *"God will generously provide all you need. Then you will always have everything you need and plenty left over to share with others."*

This is God's will for you as His beloved child. Because of His favor, you can have a life of overflowing abundance: *"…everything you need and plenty left over to share with others."*

22 DECISIONS THAT RELEASE BLESSINGS

Too often, people get the wrong idea that God's blessings are totally random and unpredictable—something they can't really do anything about. This fatalistic view keeps them from taking any *responsibility* for the life of favor God wants to give them.

Fortunately, this is not at all what the Bible teaches. God has already made HIS decision that He wants to bless His children, but now the ball is in our court—ready for OUR decision to align ourselves with the favor He wants to give us.

This principle is found throughout the Scriptures, but God makes our choice especially clear in Deuteronomy 30:15-20:

> ***See, I have set before you today life and prosperity, and death and adversity;*** *in that I command you today to love the LORD your God, to walk in His ways and to keep His commandments and His statutes and His judgments, that you may live and multiply, and* ***that the LORD your God may bless you*** *in the land where you are entering to possess it...*
>
> *I call heaven and earth to witness against you today, that I have set before you life and death,* ***the blessing and the curse.*** *So* ***choose life*** *in order that you may live, you and your descendants, by loving the LORD your God, by obeying His voice, and by holding fast to Him; for this is your life and the length of your days.*

This shouldn't really be a hard choice, because the consequences are so clear. Will you choose life or death? Do you want God's blessings or His curses?

The Lord is also telling us plainly what we must DO in order to *"choose life."* It requires a firm decision to love Him, walk in His ways, obey His voice, and hold fast to Him.

This is a decision we cannot avoid. Each of us must make a wholehearted choice to put the Lord first in our lives. Joshua described this to the Israelites when he gave them this bold challenge: *"Choose for yourselves this day whom you will serve, whether the gods which your fathers served that were on the other side of the River, or the gods of the Amorites, in whose land you dwell. But as for me and my house, we will serve the LORD"* (Joshua 24:15).

Joshua's words are packed full of meaning for your life today. You must make a choice. Instead of procrastinating, Joshua says you must choose today. There are other "gods" in our culture today, but you must turn your back on them and choose to follow the Lord instead.

Joshua declared that he had already made his choice—both for himself and for his family: *"As for me and my house, we will serve the LORD."* Are you ready to make your declaration today?

23 HOW TO BE MORE BLESSED

What if I told you there's a foolproof way to unleash a new level of blessings in your life? Would you be interested in knowing the secret? I know you would!

A story in John 13:1-17 describes just such a secret. The setting is the Passover meal Jesus celebrated with His disciples shortly before His death. Jesus had stunned the disciples by removing His robe, wrapping a towel around His waist, and washing the feet of each disciple with a basin of water. It turned out that Jesus' example of humility and servant-hood provided the disciples with a profound key for gaining more of God's favor:

> *If you want to be more blessed, the pathway is clear: Humble yourself, and learn to be a servant.*

> *After washing their feet, he put on his robe again and sat down and asked, "Do you understand what I was doing? You call me 'Teacher' and 'Lord,' and you are right, because that's what I am. And since I, your Lord and Teacher, have washed your feet, you ought to wash each other's feet. I have given you an example to follow. Do as I have done to you…Now that you know these things, God will bless you for doing them"* (vs. 12-17).

Did you catch the final line in this story—Jesus' statement in verse 17? He said, *"Now that you know these things, GOD WILL BLESS YOU for doing them."* After showing them an incredible example of what it means to be a servant—even to the extent of washing people's feet—Jesus says they should follow His example.

But a wonderful promise is included by Jesus: *"GOD **WILL** BLESS YOU."* You see, when you humble yourself and are willing to serve the Lord and other people, there's a promise attached. It's a promise of being blessed with more of God's favor and abundance.

Sadly, many people think they have to strive in their own strength to "get ahead" and climb the ladder of success. Their whole focus is on how they can receive more in life, motivating other people to serve them and meet their needs.

Yet Jesus taught that this approach is backwards. Acts 20:35 quotes Him as explaining, ***"It is more blessed to give than to receive."***

So, if you want to be more blessed, the pathway is clear: Humble yourself, and learn to be a servant. Set your focus on giving rather than receiving. When you do these things, you will be amazed at the new level of favor and blessings you'll experience.

24 TRUSTING GOD IN HARD TIMES

It's one thing to say you're trusting God when you are on the mountaintop and everything seems to be going your way. But what happens when you're stuck in the valley and God's blessings seem hard to find? Will you trust Him then?

The Bible contains numerous stories of men and women of God who had their faith tested. They had to make a decision to trust and obey the Lord, even though their breakthrough seemed distant.

I especially love the story in Genesis 26:1-14 about how Isaac sowed seeds in a time of drought and famine: *"Isaac **sowed** in that land and **reaped** in the same year a **hundredfold**. And the **LORD blessed him**, and the man **became rich**, and **continued to grow richer** until he became **very wealthy**; for he had possessions of flocks and herds and a great household, so that **the Philistines envied him**."*

I don't know about you, but many people are tempted to *hoard* their seeds during times of insecurity and lack. But not Isaac! He chose to trust God and sow seeds in the Promised Land even amid a terrible drought all around him.

What was the result of Isaac's bold step of faith and obedience? The Lord rewarded him with a gigantic harvest that was the envy of everyone around. The first year of his sowing, he received a hundredfold return. The Lord blessed him, and he became rich…continued to grow richer…and became very wealthy. In other words, the blessings in his life grew and grew as he continued to faithfully practice the law of seedtime and harvest.

Remember: You are a walking warehouse of seeds. Everything you have is either enough (your harvest), or it's the seed you must sow in order to produce your more-than-enough harvest. I encourage you to follow Isaac's example and sow seeds into God's Kingdom and the lives of others, even during your difficult seasons of life.

Perhaps you are going through a winter season in your life right now, and you don't see any way you can sow an uncommon financial seed into God's Kingdom. Yet I've discovered a surprising truth over the years: As hard as it may be, one of the surest ways to find victory in your winter season is to sow generous, sacrificial seeds.

This is something my wife Barbara and I have often done through the years. When we've had a big need, we've sown a big seed. We've seen God do amazing things in response to these simple acts of faith and obedience—not only in our own lives, but also in the lives of our friends and ministry partners.

No matter how dry and barren the fields may look around you, I'm fully confident of this: God will honor your faith…your obedience…and your expectancy. He encourages you to put His promises to the test and trust Him. He will give you a bountiful harvest from the seeds you sow into His Kingdom.

25 DRINKING FROM THE FOUNTAIN OF LIFE

The Bible describes how our actions and attitude can result in favor. But what are the keys? What do we need to do? One key is having *"good understanding,"* as we are told in Proverbs 13:15: *"Good understanding produces favor, but the way of the treacherous is hard."*

How can *"good understanding"* provide a key to releasing God's favor? The Hebrew words here reveal that this requires more than just accumulating information. It means having spiritual insight and discernment. It points to our need for good sense and for knowledge of how to succeed.

Commit yourself to studying God's Word, believing its promises, and putting it into practice.

Yet this isn't something we can achieve with a passive or apathetic attitude. It's important to actively seek wisdom and understanding—and this comes from diligently studying God's Word and putting His precepts into practice. Rather than treating God with disrespect, we need to remember that *"The fear of the LORD is the beginning of wisdom"* (Psalm 111:10).

As we revere and honor God through obeying His commandments, we embrace a lifestyle that leads to *"good understanding."* We gain God's favor and receive life-changing insights and understanding from Him. Proverbs 16:22 says this understanding is *"a fountain of life to one who has it."*

If you want to live in the favor of God, then seek His wisdom and understanding. Commit yourself to studying His Word, believing its promises, and putting it into practice. Fear God, and submit your life to Him. Seek to please Him in everything you do.

These are some of the steps that will lead you to real and lasting favor. As you follow these steps, God's favor will become a *"fountain of life"* for you, constantly refreshing you in His presence.

26 RIGHT TIME, RIGHT PLACE, RIGHT HEART

Esther seemed like an unlikely hero. She was a Hebrew orphan who lived with her Uncle Mordecai. Her people had been in captivity for over 100 years, and she was carried off against her will to the palace in Shushan, where she was placed in a house of women under the care of a eunuch named Hegai. Esther could have pouted and bemoaned her circumstances, but instead she retained a quiet and humble spirit. Rather than seeking her own will, she humbly submitted to God's plans for her life.

Esther's story would compare with a modern fairytale: A beautiful young Jewish girl torn from her homeland and taken as a captive to Persia; a tyrannical ruler who banished his queen from her royal position and initiated a search for her successor; and of course, an evil villain, Haman, who desired to perpetrate genocide against the Jews.

Even when some things don't seem to make sense, God has a plan for your victory and success.

At a pivotal moment in the history of the Jewish people, Mordecai confronted Esther with these timeless words:

> *If you remain silent at this time, relief and deliverance for the Jews will arise from another place, but you and your father's family will perish. And who knows but that you*

have come to your royal position for such a time as this?
(Esther 4:14 NIV)

Perhaps your life seems much less dramatic than Queen Esther's—but it is significant in God's sight nevertheless. Just as the Lord sovereignly orchestrated the circumstances to prepare Esther *"for such a time as this,"* so too He's weaving together the strands of your life into a beautiful tapestry to reflect His glory.

Remember today that you can trust an unknown future to an all-knowing God. For the Jewish people and for every believer today, we can be confident of this: *"He marked out their appointed times in history"* (Acts 17:26 NIV).

God has placed you in this time in history, my friend. He has orchestrated your circumstances and experiences to prepare you to carry out His purposes. And now it's your time to *shine!*

Even when some things don't seem to make sense, God has a plan for your victory and success (Jeremiah 29:11). He has a happy ending in mind for YOUR story, just as He accomplished for Esther!

27 THE FRAGRANCE OF GOD'S FAVOR

Esther's Hebrew name was Hadassah, derived from the word for "myrtle." She was aptly named, for the leaves of a myrtle tree only release their fragrance when they are crushed.

When you're living in the favor of God, the Bible says your life will emit the sweet fragrance of Christ. Paul described this as an "exquisite fragrance" and "sweet scent" that should permeate the atmosphere wherever we go: *"Everywhere we go, people breathe in the exquisite fragrance. Because of Christ, we give off a sweet scent"* (2 Corinthians 2:14-15 MSG).

Is that the kind of life you are living right now? Can people smell the fragrance of Christ—the fragrance of God's favor—or are you giving off the putrid aroma of religiosity, pride, or bitterness?

Esther could have been bitter about losing her parents and living in a foreign land, but instead she imparted a positive, cheerful attitude even in stressful circumstances. When challenged by Mordecai to take action, Esther's only request was that the Jews gather together to fast and pray with her and her handmaidens. Her response to Mordecai was a

When Esther made her request known to the king, she recognized that the answer would require "favor" in his sight.

magnificent display of humility and obedience:

> *Go, gather together all the Jews who are in Susa, and fast for me…I and my attendants will fast as you do. When this is done, I will go to the king, even though it is against the law. And if I perish, I perish* (Esther 4:16 NIV).

You may need to battle for your breakthrough, but victory is assured when you obey the Lord and walk in His favor.

Trusting in God's favor and protection, Esther was willing even to perish in order to save her people from destruction. On the third day, she dressed in her most beautiful gown and stepped confidently into the throne room. Seeing his beautiful queen slip into the hall pleased the King Ahasuerus, and he extended his golden scepter in her direction.

My friend, this is a beautiful picture of how King Jesus is extending His hand to you today, inviting you to come and bring Him your requests. But you need to come into His throne room boldly rather than timidly: *"Let us come boldly to the throne of our gracious God…and we will find grace to help us when we need it most"* (Hebrews 4:16 NLT).

When Esther made her request known to the king, she recognized that the answer would require *"favor"* in his sight:

> *If I have **found favor** with you, Your Majesty, and if it pleases you, grant me my life—this is my petition. And spare my people—this is my request. For I and my people have been sold to be destroyed, killed and annihilated* (Esther 7:3-4 NIV).

King Ahasuerus was stunned! Who would dare threaten the queen and her people? Esther pointed a finger at the culprit: *"An adversary and enemy! This vile Haman!"* (Esther 7:6 NIV)

Friend, there are two principles here that apply to your life today: As believers, Satan is our sworn *"adversary and enemy."* The Bible makes this clear: *"Your adversary the devil walks about like a roaring lion, seeking whom he may devour. Resist him, steadfast in the faith"* (1 Peter 5:8-9).

But the fact that we're in a spiritual battle is not meant to scare us—God simply wants to *prepare us.* Just as Haman was eventually exposed and defeated, we are destined to overcome the devil in Jesus' mighty name. You may need to *battle* for your breakthrough, but victory is assured when you obey the Lord and walk in His favor.

28 DON'T SKIP FORGIVENESS

Mark 2:1-12 (NASB) tells the intriguing story of a paralyzed man who was carried to Jesus by four faithful friends. This was no easy task. Jesus was preaching the Word in a house packed so full of people that these men were unable to get the paralyzed man to Jesus.

But these men weren't going to be denied. They climbed up on the roof of the house, dug a hole in the roof, and lowered the man's pallet right in front of Jesus.

Whether you are feeling "stuck" in your emotions, finances, career, relationships, or some other area, God can set you free as you take a step of faith.

The man had obviously come in search of a healing for his paralysis. So the crowd must have been shocked when Jesus addressed an entirely different issue in the paralyzed man's life: *"Son, your sins are forgiven"* (v. 5).

Doesn't this seem like a strange statement at first? Couldn't Jesus see that the man was *paralyzed?* He hadn't come in search of eternal salvation but for a healing of his body.

When you bring your prayer request to the Lord today, don't be surprised if He addresses an issue you didn't even have on your prayer list. You see, this paralyzed man had a spiritual issue—an issue of forgiveness—that Jesus needed to deal with before addressing the physical paralysis.

My friend, let's be clear: Jesus eventually wants to deal with *every* issue in your life. When He died on the Cross, He purchased not only your forgiveness, but also the healing of your emotions and your body (Isaiah 53:3-6).

Jesus pointed this out when He told the skeptics surrounding the paralyzed man: *"Which is easier, to say to the paralytic, 'Your sins are forgiven'; or to say, 'Get up, and pick up your pallet and walk'?"* (v. 9) But in the case of the paralyzed man, Jesus chose to deal with the forgiveness issue first.

But then Jesus said something to the man that must have seemed outrageous on its face: *"I say to you, get up, pick up your pallet and go home"* (v. 11). He told a paralyzed man to do the one thing that seemed totally IMPOSSIBLE for him to do: Jesus told him to walk!

How does all of this apply to *your* life today? First, you need to be open to the possibility that God wants to deal with a *deeper* issue in your life than the issue that seems so pressing right now. Once He has addressed that issue and brought you to a place of repentance, forgiveness, and restoration, He is likely to tell you to take an "impossible" step of faith.

No matter how difficult your circumstances may seem today, you can experience a turnaround through the favor of God.

You may not be suffering from physical paralysis like the man in this story, but He wants to free you from any other form of paralysis that may be holding you back. This is such good news! Whether you are feeling "stuck" in your emotions, finances, career, relationships, or some other area, God can set you free as you take a step of faith—as "impossible" as it might seem.

This man obeyed Jesus' command and walked away from his paralysis. And I love how this impacted the onlookers that day. Totally amazed, they glorified God and said, *"We have never seen anything like this"* (v. 12).

No matter how difficult your circumstances may seem today. You can experience a turnaround through the favor of God. So make sure you aren't allowing your past control your *future*. The Lord wants to do things in your life that you've *never seen before!*

THE LAND OF 'MORE THAN ENOUGH'

Prosperity is one of the characteristics of living in God's favor. It's heartbreaking that so many Believers are living the land of "Never Enough" or "Barely Enough," when the Lord wants to move His children into the land of "MORE Than Enough."

This powerful principle is found throughout the Bible, but I want to focus now on an amazing promise from God in Malachi 3:8-12:

> "Will a man rob God? Yet you have robbed Me! But you say, 'In what way have we robbed You?' In tithes and offerings. You are cursed with a curse, for you have robbed Me, even this whole nation. Bring all the tithes into the storehouse, that there may be food in My house, and try Me now in this," says the LORD of hosts, "If I will not open for you the windows of heaven and pour out for you such blessing that there will not be room enough to receive it. And I will rebuke the devourer for your sakes, so that he will not destroy the fruit of your ground, nor shall the vine fail to bear fruit for you in the field," says the LORD of hosts; "and all nations will call you blessed, for you will be a delightful land."

God's message here is packed with meaning that can change your life. First, He tells His people they've forfeited His blessings because of their failure to bring Him their tithes and offerings. This was no small matter, because God warns that they were *"cursed with a curse"* due to their unfaithfulness in this area.

But then the Lord shares an awesome picture of the abundant prosperity we can have when we are faithful and generous in our giving. In fact, He invites us to TEST Him in this promise!

For those who faithfully bring their tithes and special offerings into God's Kingdom storehouse, He promises to literally open *"the windows of heaven"* to pour out His abundant blessings. Instead of giving us just barely enough to meet our needs, the Lord says He will pour out *"such blessing that there will not be room enough to receive it."*

In other words, God wants to give us blessings that *overflow*, with *more than enough* for our needs. As we're promised in Genesis 12:2, we'll not only be blessed in our own lives, but God will also give us enough to become a blessing to others.

This passage in Malachi 3 also says God will *"rebuke the devourer"* for our sakes. Do you see how significant this is? John 10:10 tells us that the devil is a thief who comes to steal, kill, and destroy God's blessings in our lives. John 10:10 also says Jesus wants to give us an abundant life, so we need to find out how we can overcome the *"thief"* along the way.

When you're faithful in your stewardship and walk in a covenant relationship with Him, the Lord Himself will rebuke the enemy and keep him from devouring your blessings!

God provides the answer in Malachi 3. When we're faithful in our stewardship and walk in a covenant relationship with Him, *the Lord Himself* will rebuke the enemy and keep him from devouring our blessings! Isn't that good news?

Notice that Malachi 3:11 describes *"the fruit of your ground"* as part of God's favor toward those who obey Him in tithes and special offerings. In other words, He is promising an *abundant harvest*—but this promise only is relevant for those who have first been faithful to sow SEEDS into His Kingdom!

I pray today that you are ready to leave the land of Never Enough or the land of Barely Enough. When you put these principles of God's Word into action, He will give you overflowing abundance in the land of More Than Enough!

30 SQUANDERED FAVOR

No one who has ever lived has experienced the kind of supernatural favor God gave Adam and Eve in the Garden of Eden. We can only imagine what it must have been like: a perfect climate and pristine environment, abundant food, no poverty or lack, harmony with the animals, no sickness or death, and the absence of strife with one another.

But all that changed when Adam and Eve sinned in Genesis 3. Because of the Lord's incredible favor in their lives, they already "had it all." But the devil used the serpent to seduce them into doubting God's love for them. He implied that God was trying to withhold something good from them by commanding them not to eat the forbidden fruit. All the while, God had given them this commandment for their own good.

Disobedience changed everything for Adam and Eve. Their Heavenly Father had created them for abundance and blessings, but now they were experiencing fear, frustration, and curses instead.

It was a traumatic turn of events, to say the least. But God explained to Adam how his sin had caused divine favor to be squandered:

> *To Adam He said, "Because you have heeded the voice of your*
> *wife, and have eaten from the tree of which I commanded*
> *you, saying, 'You shall not eat of it':*

"Cursed is the ground for your sake;
In toil you shall eat of it
All the days of your life.

"Both thorns and thistles it shall bring forth for you,
And you shall eat the herb of the field.

"In the sweat of your face you shall eat bread
Till you return to the ground,
For out of it you were taken;
For dust you are,
And to dust you shall return" (vs. 17-19).

What a tragic outcome! Instead of being blessed, the ground was cursed. Instead of crops in abundance, thorns and thistles would spring up. Instead of automatically enjoying God's provision, Adam would only make ends meet by his sweat and hard work. And instead of living forever, death became part of the human experience.

However, we learn in the New Testament that God has reversed the curse (Galatians 3:13-14). Through Christ's work on the Cross, the squandered favor has been restored to humankind when we repent of our sins and turn to Him in faith.

Disobedience changed everything for Adam and Eve.

You don't have to listen to the devil's lies anymore, my friend. God LOVES you, and He wants to restore you to all the favor Adam lost. Make a fresh commitment today to trust the Lord and obey His instructions. Every curse will be broken, and you can regain everything the enemy has stolen from you!

31 WHEN FAVOR BREAKS THROUGH

Isaiah 58 is an intriguing chapter about some steps Believers can take to unleash more of God's favor in their lives. It was written at a time when God's people needed to acknowledge their sins and return to Him with repentance, prayer, and fasting. Yet the Lord was pointing out that even when they went through the motions of prayer and fasting, they sometimes missed the point—and also missed out on the incredible blessings available.

"Is this not the fast that I have chosen," God asks in verse 6, *"To loose the bonds of wickedness, to undo the heavy burdens, to let the oppressed go free, and that you break every yoke?"* There are two parts of the Lord's message here: First, He was challenging His people to release their servants from heavy burdens and oppression. But the second message here is that He wants to release us from OUR burdens when we humble ourselves and obey Him.

The chapter describes God's amazing favor being released when we care for the poor and share our bread with the hungry: *"Then your light shall break forth like the morning, your healing shall spring forth speedily, and your righteousness shall go before you; the glory of the LORD shall be your rear guard"* (vs. 7-8).

God also promises us a new level of answered prayer and spiritual impact: *"Then you shall call, and the LORD will answer; you shall cry, and He will say, 'Here I am'... Then your light shall dawn in the darkness, and your darkness shall be as the noonday"* (v. 9).

This favor will also result in a new dimension of God's guidance, provision, and strength: *"The LORD will guide you continually, and satisfy your soul in drought, and strengthen your bones; you shall be like a watered garden, and like a spring of water, whose waters do not fail"* (v. 11).

The chapter ends with God's promise when we delight ourselves in Him: *"I will cause you to ride on the high hills of the earth, and feed you with the heritage of Jacob your father"* (v. 14). You see, my friend, when you delight in Him, He will lift you up. His light…His glory…His favor… and His healing power will spring forth in greater magnitude than you've ever experienced before.

This favor will result in a new dimension of God's guidance, provision, and strength.

I encourage you to read Isaiah 58 for yourself, from start to finish. Pay special attention to God's *principles* and His *promises*. The chapter paints a beautiful picture of what a life of favor looks like. This is the amazing, supernatural life God wants to give YOU, my friend.

32 PROVISION IN DIFFICULT TIMES

I love the story in 1 Kings 17:8-16 where God provided for a widow and her son in a most unusual way. The story begins when the prophet Elijah was sent by God to the town of Zarephath. There was a terrible drought and famine in the land, and God told Elijah he would meet a widow there who would provide for his needs.

When Elijah received this word from God, he must have thought, "This is wonderful. The Lord is sending me to a rich widow who has plenty of food and resources to provide for me." However, when he found the widow, she and her son were one meal away from starving to death! She was in a season of life that seemed totally hopeless. Perhaps you can relate.

When Elijah asked this impoverished widow for a piece of bread, she replied:

As the LORD your God lives, I have no bread, only a handful of flour in the bowl and a little oil in the jar; and behold, I am gathering a few sticks that I may go in and prepare for me and my son, that we may eat it and die (v. 12).

At this point, Elijah might have thought, "Wow. Maybe this isn't the correct widow! I surely can't ask her for anything, when she and her son are destitute."

But instead of backing down from his request, the prophet

of God told the woman: *"Do not fear; go, do as you have said, but make me a little bread cake from it first and bring it out to me, and afterward you may make one for yourself and for your son. For thus says the LORD God of Israel, "The bowl of flour shall not be exhausted, nor shall the jar of oil be empty, until the day that the LORD sends rain on the face of the earth"* (vs. 13-14).

The widow must have wondered if Elijah was crazy. However, since she was going to die anyway unless God did a miracle, her desperation overcame any skepticism. We read in verses 15 and 16:

*So she went and **did** according to the word of Elijah, and she and he and her household ate for many days. The bowl of flour was not exhausted nor did the jar of oil become empty, according to the word of the LORD which He spoke through Elijah.*

What a great example of someone who sowed a seed during a time of incredible lack! As a result, the widow miraculously received an incredible release of prosperity and blessing from the Lord. She and her son *"ate for many days"* on that handful of flour and small amount of oil! As this faithful woman obeyed the word from God's prophet, she and her household received a harvest of supernatural abundance.

Friend, I don't know your circumstances today. But God does. He also knows the seed in your hand, and the abundant harvest He wants to give you.

As you trust the Lord with your possessions and take a step of faith, this could be the day that things begin to turn around for you. God's favor is closer than you think!

Sometimes people are simply too proud to recognize their need for God's forgiveness and favor. It's hard to believe that some people don't feel any need for God to forgive them, but it's more common than you think. Jesus told a story about this in Luke 18:9-14:

> *Two men went up to the temple to pray, one a Pharisee and the other a tax collector. The Pharisee stood and prayed thus with himself, "God, I thank You that I am not like other men—extortioners, unjust, adulterers, or even as this tax collector. I fast twice a week; I give tithes of all that I possess."*

> *And the tax collector, standing afar off, would not so much as raise his eyes to heaven, but beat his breast, saying, "God, be merciful to me a sinner!" I tell you, this man went down to his house justified rather than the other; for everyone who exalts himself will be humbled, and he who humbles himself will be exalted.*

This story provides quite a contrast in how people see their need for God's forgiveness. The Pharisee was a respected religious leader who saw no need for God to forgive him. He compared himself to other people and concluded that he was already more righteous than they were.

Friend, this approach never works. You can't receive God's favor by comparing yourself to others and feeling like you are more worthy than they are.

The tax collector, in contrast, accurately recognized his need for God's mercy and forgiveness. He readily acknowledged that he was a sinner in need of a Savior. And Jesus ends the story by saying this man is the one who was right with God, positioned to receive the Lord's mercy, grace, and favor.

And I don't want you to miss this final line: *"Everyone who exalts himself will be humbled, and he who humbles himself will be exalted."* You see, it takes *humility* to admit our need for God's forgiveness. But Jesus promises here that if we are willing to humble ourselves, God will surely exalt us and lift us up!

Jesus promises that if you are willing to humble yourself, God will surely exalt you and lift you up!

Friend, my prayer is that you are already walking in God's favor and experiencing the abundant life Jesus promised. But if you're not, I encourage you to take time today to come into God's presence and ask Him to show you the condition of your heart.

Are there still sins you need to confess? Do you still need to be forgiven and cleansed? Or have you been living with unnecessary guilt or condemnation, even after the Lord has forgiven you?

I'm convinced God is ready to pour His supernatural favor into your life. Are you ready to humble yourself and admit how much you need His grace and favor?

34 RESTLESS WANDERING

Because of their disobedience to God, Adam and Eve not only forfeited God's favor in their own lives, but they also impacted humankind for the rest of history. We see these tragic consequences in the lives of their children, Cain and Abel.

Each of these two young men brought offerings to the Lord, but their offerings were quite different: *"Cain brought some of the fruits of the soil as an offering to the LORD. And Abel also brought an offering—fat portions from some of the firstborn of his flock"* (Genesis 4:3-4 NIV).

On the surface, both of these offerings probably seemed sincere enough. Yet God was pleased with one, and rejected the other: *"The LORD looked with favor on Abel and his offering, but on Cain and his offering he did not look with favor"* (v. 5).

What was there about Abel's offering that unleashed God's favor? And why did the Lord reject the offering brought by Cain?

The answer is found in this principle woven throughout the Scriptures: *"Without the shedding of blood there is no forgiveness"* (Hebrews 9:22 NIV). This is first seen in Genesis 3:6-21. After Adam and Eve sinned, they attempted to cover themselves by sewing fig leaves together, an approach later reflected by Cain's offering of his crops. In contrast, God made *"garments of skin"* for Adam and Eve—an act that required an animal sacrifice and the shedding of blood. This was reflected in Abel's blood sacrifice, and ultimately by Jesus' death for us on the Cross.

When Cain saw he didn't have the favor of the Lord, he could have repented and sought God's forgiveness. But instead, he just became stubborn, angry, and depressed: *"So Cain was very angry, and his face was downcast"* (Genesis 4:5). Even after this initial response, God gave him an opportunity to *"do what is right"* (v. 6), but Cain refused.

Without God's forgiveness or favor, Cain's life spiraled out of control. He killed his brother, an act that caused him to reap even more of a curse than he had inherited from his parents. He ended up becoming *"a restless wanderer on the earth"* (v. 12).

Friend, God doesn't want you or me to be restless wanderers. He wants us to come to Him in faith, based on the shed blood of His Son Jesus. As we come to Him on the basis of that perfect sacrifice, we can be confident of His favor. We can let go of our stubbornness, anger, and depression. And instead of aimless wandering, we can fulfill God's purpose for our life.

Instead of aimless wandering, you can fulfill God's purpose for your life.

It's not too late for your turnaround! Why not take a step of faith and get started today?

35 REVERSING NEGATIVE CIRCUMSTANCES

Every one of us has faced negative circumstances at one time or another in our lives. Perhaps you are in the midst of negative situations right now.

Sometimes we encounter adverse circumstances because of bad decisions we've made in the past. Most of us have suffered in our health, finances, emotions, or relationships because of foolish choices that grieved the heart of God.

However, at other times, we face bewildering circumstances through no fault of our own. These are just the storms and winter seasons that are a part of life. Jesus taught that our loving Heavenly Father *"sends rain on the just and on the unjust"* (Matthew 5:45). In other words, some trials and tribulations are simply a part of the human condition, regardless of whether we are walking in God's favor or not.

Your plague may not be the same kind David faced in 1 Chronicles 21, but perhaps it's a broken relationship, an illness, a problem with your children, an addiction, or a financial setback.

However, the Bible illustrates that faith and obedience often can reverse the negative circumstances that have undercut God's favor in your life. First Chronicles 21 tells the story of King David's sin in doing a census to determine the strength of his troops—even after he was warned that this would grieve the Lord.

God was angry at this and gave David the choice of three different consequences for his transgression. Each of these proposed judgments from God were severe, and David chose the option of three days of plague upon the nation. This plague was so harsh that in a short time 70,000 people died. But as the angel of the Lord was about to destroy the city of Jerusalem, the calamity was suddenly averted.

How was the severe tide of divine judgment turned? What can we learn from David's example in seeking God's mercy and finding the favor of the Lord once again?

As you take bold steps of faith and obedience, the Lord will restore His favor and blessings in your life.

God's angel tells David in verse 18 to *"build an altar to the LORD on the threshing floor of Ornan the Jebusite."* David obeys this word of instruction, and in verse 22 he says to Ornan, the owner of the threshing floor: *"Give me the site of this threshing floor, that I may build on it an altar to the LORD; for the **full price** you shall give it to me, that the plague may be restrained from the people."*

Although Ornan tells David he can have the land for free, the king refuses this generous offer. David's response may seem surprising to you, but look at his explanation in verse 24: *"No, but I will surely buy it for the **full price**; for I will not take what is yours for the LORD, or offer a burnt offering which **costs me nothing**."*

David's example should be a great lesson for us today. He refused to give an offering to the Lord that cost him nothing! True worship always will cost us something! Our offerings are seeds, and unless they're precious to us, they won't be precious to God either. He will never be pleased with our leftovers.

As David gave his sacrificial offering to the Lord, the plague suddenly stopped! We read in verse 27: *"The LORD commanded the angel, and he put his sword back in its sheath."*

Perhaps you're facing a "plague" of negative circumstances today. Your plague may not be the same kind David faced in 1 Chronicles 21, but perhaps it's a broken relationship, an illness, a problem with your children, an addiction, or a financial setback.

If you are under some kind of attack like this today, I encourage you to follow David's example and place your sacrificial offering on God's altar. As you take bold steps of faith and obedience, I'm convinced the Lord will restore His favor and blessings in your life.

36 FROM PAIN TO PROMISE

We all go through painful experiences of one kind or another, and how we *handle* life's adversities will have a lot to do in determining our character and our destiny. The intriguing story of Jabez reveals how our pain can be transformed as we lay hold of God's promises:

Jabez was more honorable than his brothers; and his mother called his name Jabez, saying, "Because I bore him in pain." Jabez called upon the God of Israel, saying, "Oh that you would bless me and enlarge my border, and that your hand might be with me, and that you would keep me from harm so that it might not bring me pain!" And God granted what he asked (1 Chronicles 4:9-10 ESV).

Too often, people assume that their upbringing inevitably determines their destiny. But Jabez knew otherwise. Right from the beginning, we see that he stood out from the crowd, and he was *"more honorable"* even than his own brothers.

However, as we read about Jabez' life, we realize his life got off to a rough start. It seemed like the cards were stacked against him. His birth was so painful that *"his mother called his name Jabez"*—derived from the Hebrew word for *pain*.

Perhaps you can relate to Jabez' story at this point. Your parents probably didn't name you "a Pain"—at least not formally! But let's be honest: Sometimes parents, siblings, peers, pastors, or employers send us negative messages about our identity...who we are. Or maybe there was a bully in your neighborhood who said you were too skinny...too fat...too ugly...too short...or too stupid.

There's an old saying that is totally false. I'm sure you've heard it: "Sticks and stones can break my bones, but words can never hurt me." That truth is just the opposite: We can recover from sticks and stones and even broken bones—but people's words often cause us a lifetime of hurt.

Just as God did in the life of Jabez, He has planned a happy ending for YOU!

That's how Jabez' story begins: with pain...with rejection from the very people who should have shown him the most love and acceptance. But the good news is that Jabez wasn't content to wallow in his situation. He rejected the labels put on him by his detractors, choosing instead to seek God for a new identity...a new purpose...and a new destiny.

How did your story begin in its early chapters? Perhaps you had a wonderful, loving family that cared for you and nurtured you all along the way. But I meet so many people today who have had an experience more like Jabez.

So what did Jabez *do* to break free from the negative labels that threatened to bind him to a life of failure or mediocrity? The text says, *"Jabez called upon the God of Israel."* If you are going to break free from people's opinions about you, you must cry out for HIGHER opinion—the opinion of Almighty God. In the end, it's really just HIS opinion that matters, isn't it? When you stand before Him in eternity, the bullies and naysayers won't be there to tear you down. The only thing that will matter will be hear

His beautiful words of affirmation, *"Well done, good and faithful servant"* (Matthew 25:21).

We're specifically told that he called upon *"the God of Israel."* This doesn't just mean he was calling upon the God of the nation of Israel. No, Jabez was calling upon the God of JACOB—the patriarch whose name was changed by God to ISRAEL.

Do you see why this is significant? Jacob had a pretty dysfunctional childhood, and his own brother seemed intent on killing him. And just like Jabez, Jacob had been given a rather negative name—Jacob, the "supplanter" or "usurper." And up until the point when Jacob's name was changed, he had lived up to his negative name, becoming an opportunistic scoundrel and deceiver.

But after Jacob wrestled all night with God in Genesis 32:22-29, the Lord changed his name to Israel, which meant "Triumphant with God" or "Prince with God."

You see, Jabez knew the story of Jacob well. He saw how God had transformed Jacob from being a PAIN to being a PRINCE. And Jabez called on the *"God of Israel (Jacob)"* to do the same for him.

Perhaps you need a name change today...a new identity. God can take your PAIN and make you a PRINCE or PRINCESS. He can take your FAILURES and give you a glorious FUTURE. But you have a role to play. You must cry out to Him, like Jabez did. You may even need to wrestle with Him, as Jacob did. But don't let go until you have a new name...a fresh start... a new beginning.

And I want you to notice that Jabez asked God to give him several specific things. This is an important lesson for us, because sometimes our prayers and our plans are too vague and undefined. I encourage you today to be *specific* about what you are asking God for. Specific prayer requests will bring specific answers!

Jabez first requested of the Lord, *"Oh that you would bless me."* God wants to bless YOU, my friend! So go ahead, like Jabez, and ASK Him to bless you.

The second thing Jabez asked is that God would *"enlarge his border."* In the same way, God wants to enlarge you today. He wants to give you bigger dreams…higher vision…more audacious plans.

But think of how incredible this prayer request must have been for Jabez, the man who was labeled a pain and a loser. He could have curled up in a ball and wallowed in his victim-hood, but instead he did just the opposite. He called on God to enlarge his territory and give him greater responsibilities and impact.

So what about YOU? Is there some area of your life that you need God to enlarge? Your career…your finances…your health…your relationships…your ministry…your vision? Today can be your first step in asking God for an INCREASE that will change your entire trajectory in life.

Jabez' next request was that *"God's hand"* would be upon his life. This expressed Jabez' recognition that he needed GOD'S FAVOR in order to accomplish his life's PURPOSE. This is so important for you to see: In order to escape from any painful experiences that would hold you back from your destiny, *you need God's favor.*

Jabez' final request was that God would keep him from harm—from the things that would cause pain, either to himself or the people around him. Jabez was a man of great faith, but he also was a realist. He understood that he had received a legacy of pain and dysfunction, and the natural thing would be to continue that legacy in his own life. It's no secret that people in pain tend to cause pain to others. People who have been abused often become abusers. Children of alcoholics and addicts too often follow in their parents' footsteps.

But Jabez knew the negative patterns must STOP! He had been called a *pain*, but that's not how he wanted to treat others.

This passage about Jabez ends with a beautiful conclusion: *"And God granted what he asked."* I love happy endings, don't you? Just as God did in the life of Jabez, He has planned a happy ending for YOU!

37 FORGIVING THE INEXCUSABLE

In order to fully walk in the supernatural favor of God, it's necessary both to receive His forgiveness and to extend it others. Forgiveness is not optional if you want to experience God's abundant blessings. The Bible is clear: God *commands* us to forgive those who have wronged us, and this is a vital key to unlocking His blessings and favor in our lives.

Author C.S. Lewis once said, "To be a Christian means to forgive the inexcusable, because God has forgiven the inexcusable in you." And G.K. Chesterton wrote, "To love means loving the unlovable. To forgive means pardoning the unpardonable."

This is far from easy. In fact, it often seems humanly impossible. You see, we need *God's help* if we are going to forgive other people as He has forgiven us.

When Jesus taught His disciples to pray in Matthew 6:9-13, He included many important insights. We are to approach God as our loving Heavenly Father, not as a stern Judge who is unconcerned about our needs. We are told to pray for His Kingdom to come and His will to be done, on earth as it is in Heaven. Jesus also instructed us to pray for God to provide our *"daily bread."*

But then He focused squarely on the issue of forgiveness. Verse 12 says, *"Forgive us our sins, as we have forgiven those who sin against us."* Do you see how important this is? We need to receive God's forgiveness, and we also need to forgive anyone who has wronged us.

The Lord's Prayer in Matthew 6 is a beautiful picture of living in God's favor and abundance. However, don't miss the crucial ingredient of forgiveness. If you're not experiencing God's forgiveness, you won't experience His favor either. And His favor will also be blocked if you refuse to forgive others.

In addition, Jesus linked the forgiveness issue to answered prayer. He said in Mark 11:24-25, *"Whatever you ask for in prayer, believe that you have received it, and it will be yours. And when you stand praying, if you hold anything against anyone, forgive them, so that your Father in heaven may forgive you your sins."*

> *If you're not experiencing God's forgiveness, you won't experience His favor either.*

Friend, your Heavenly Father loves you. He wants to meet your needs and answer your prayers. But first you need to make sure you have received His forgiveness and been willing to forgive anyone who has wronged you. When you do these two things, get ready for an outbreak of supernatural favor in your life!

38 ENRICHED IN EVERYTHING

It's impossible to fully unlock God's favor in your life without understanding and applying the incredible principle of seedtime and harvest. This powerful law goes clear back to the beginning of time, and Genesis 8:22 promises that it will stay in effect as long as the earth remains.

The Bible teaches that our Heavenly Father wants us to have an abundant harvest of His blessings—so much so that He even provides us with the *seeds!* The apostle Paul writes about this in 2 Corinthians 9:10-11:

> *He who **supplies seed to the sower** and bread for food will supply and multiply your seed for sowing and increase the harvest of your righteousness; you will be **enriched in everything** for all liberality, which through us is producing thanksgiving to God* (2 Corinthians 9:10-11 NASB).

Notice that this passage doesn't say God provides seeds to *everyone*—it says He supplies those who are *sowers*. This means the best way to experience God's financial favor is to set your heart on sowing financial seeds into His Kingdom. If you do, He will first supply you seeds, and then He will provide you with a harvest from the seeds you sow.

However, it's very important to realize that the promise in this scripture isn't limited to finances. It says that faithful sowers will be *"enriched in EVERYTHING."* Isn't that awesome?

Whatever your need is today—whether financial pressures, a broken relationship, an illness, an addiction, or problems on your job — God will miraculously step into your circumstances when you take a step of faith and sow your seed!

God takes the seed you've released from your hand and then gives you wonderful harvests from His hand.

Remember: When you sow a seed into God's Kingdom, it doesn't leave your life. God takes the seed you've released from YOUR hand and then gives you wonderful harvests from HIS hand.

Jesus makes an incredible promise about this principle in Luke 6:38, *"Give, and it will be given to you. A good measure, pressed down, shaken together and running over, will be poured into your lap. For with the measure you use, it will be measured to you."*

This is wonderful news, isn't it? Not only does the Lord promise that you will personally receive a harvest from what you give, but also He says it will *overflow* and *run over*—blessing others as well.

Through the law of seedtime and harvest, you can have a life of overflowing abundance, my friend. You will be enriched not just financially, but *"in everything."*

39 FINDING FAVOR IN GOD'S EYES

Genesis 6 describes a bleak situation on planet Earth. This was quite a contrast to God's original creation, when He saw all that He had made, *"and it was very good"* (Genesis 1:31).

Humankind had become so corrupt that God made a radical decision:

> *The LORD saw how great the wickedness of the human race had become on the earth, and that every inclination of the thoughts of the human heart was only evil all the time. The LORD regretted that he had made human beings on the earth, and his heart was deeply troubled. So the LORD said, "I will wipe from the face of the earth the human race I have created—and with them the animals, the birds and the creatures that move along the ground—for I regret that I have made them"* (Genesis 6:5-7 NIV).

It's hard to imagine more dreadful circumstances, and God wasn't going to put up with this pervasive wickedness any longer. Humankind seemed on the brink of forfeiting God's favor forever.

However, verse 8 reveals God's plan to turn things around: *"But Noah found favor in the eyes of the LORD."* When all hope for humanity seemed lost, God spotted a solitary man He could show His grace and favor to.

Why did the Lord choose Noah out of all the other people on the earth? Even though we don't know all the reasons, we're given some important clues: *"Noah was a righteous man, blameless among the people of his time, and he walked faithfully with God"* (v. 9).

Just as the Bible predicted long ago, we're living today in an evil age not much different than *"the days of Noah"* (Luke 17:26). So the question is this: Will we walk faithfully with God as Noah did? Will we be righteous and blameless, standing out among the other people in our society?

When all hope for humanity seemed lost, God spotted a solitary man He could show His grace and favor to.

It has never been more urgent for God's people to walk closely with Him and find favor in His eyes. As the Bible described, we live in a time when *"darkness covers the earth and thick darkness the peoples"* (Isaiah 60:1-2 NIV). Our mandate from God is clear: *"Arise, shine, for your light has come, and the glory of the LORD rises upon you...his glory appears over you."*

As the world gets darker, the light of God's people must shine brighter. As evil abounds, the Lord's grace and favor must abound even more (Romans 5:20).

Things may look dark and hopeless all around you today, but don't despair. It's time for you to arise and shine! Like Noah, you can find favor in the eyes of the Lord—and that will change *everything*.

40 FROM FRUSTRATION TO FAVOR

Have you ever had a frustrating day, when nothing seemed to go right? Perhaps you worked hard on some project or relationship, but the results were dismal nevertheless.

Some of Jesus' first disciples were fishermen, and they experienced this kind of frustration when they *"worked hard all night"* without catching any fish (Luke 5:5 NIV). Maybe you're facing a similar situation today. You've tried hard and done your best, but you've come up empty.

Fortunately, Jesus didn't leave these fishermen to wallow in defeat and frustration. He had a plan to give them a breakthrough, just as He has a wonderful plan to turn things around for YOU today.

Jesus gave these men a clear word of instruction: *"Put out into deep water, and let down your nets for a catch"* (v. 4). They were resistant at first, not seeing how it would do much good to change the position of their nets at this point. But then Peter answered, *"Because you say so, I will let down the nets"* (v. 5).

If you've been dealing with a frustrating situation, pause for a few moments and ask yourself: Has Jesus given you any instructions for how to receive your breakthrough? This may seem small or inconsequential, but it's the key you need for unleashing God's favor in your life.

If you haven't heard His instructions yet, make sure you are quieting your heart and listening for His voice. Also make sure you are fully surrendered to Him, willing to obey His instructions when they come.

Despite their skepticism, Peter and the other fishermen chose to obey Jesus and follow His advice. The turnaround was immediate: *"They caught such a large number of fish that their nets began to break"* (v. 6).

Wow. After catching nothing the previous night, a stunning breakthrough came when they obeyed Jesus' instructions.

Friend, I'm convinced today your breakthrough may be much closer than you think. No matter how frustrating your past struggles may have been, a new day is here as you follow Jesus' instructions and *"let down your nets for a catch."*

No matter how frustrating your past struggles may have been, a new day is here as you follow Jesus' instructions.

Remember: God is *"able to do immeasurably more than all we ask or imagine, according to his power that is at work within us"* (Ephesians 3:20 NIV). He will replace your frustration with FAVOR!

41

ENCOUNTERING JEHOVAH-JIREH

Perhaps you've sung worship songs or heard preachers that refer to God as Jehovah-Jireh, which means "the Lord will provide." This is a beautiful description of an important aspect of the Lord's favor, but it came about in a very unusual story told in Genesis 22.

Isaac, Abraham and Sarah's long-awaited child of promise, had finally arrived. I'm sure they were overjoyed by this miraculous birth when their bodies seemed well past the age of child-bearing.

Then horror came, as God told Abraham, *"Take now your son, your only son Isaac, whom you love, and go to the land of Moriah, and offer him there as a burnt offering on one of the mountains of which I shall tell you"* (Genesis 22:2).

This was the ultimate test, for Abraham loved Isaac more than life itself. Yet he was committed to a life of obedience, and he trusted God to bless that obedience. Although Abraham must have wondered why the Lord would demand such a thing, we're told in Hebrews 11:17: *"By faith Abraham, when he was tested, offered up Isaac."*

Although today we can read the story of Abraham's willingness to sacrifice Isaac and see it had a happy ending, Abraham didn't have that benefit. He just knew what God was asking him to do—and he obeyed without question or protest. He could have argued…hesitated…or tried to bargain with God. But he didn't.

However, puzzled about God's plan, his heart must have been heavy as he set out on the three-day journey to Mount Moriah. Yet there are signs that God already had convinced Abraham that Isaac would either be spared or would be raised from the dead, if necessary (Hebrews 11:19). That's why Abraham could assure his son, *"God himself will provide the lamb for the burnt offering"* (Genesis 22:8 NIV).

After Abraham showed his willingness to put Isaac on the altar, the Lord told him:

> ***Because you have done this*** *and have not withheld your son, your only son, I will surely **bless you** and make your descendants as numerous as the stars in the sky and as the sand on the seashore. Your descendants will take possession of the cities of their enemies, and through your offspring all nations on earth will be blessed, because you have obeyed me* (Genesis 22:16-18 NIV).

What a stunning lesson on the blessings of obedience. Although God doesn't always let us know ahead of time HOW He will bless our obedience, we can be confident that He WILL bless us with his supernatural favor in some way.

When Abraham obeyed God by putting Isaac on the altar, he probably had no clue on *how* God would provide. Would the Lord grant a last-minute stay of execution? Would He raise Isaac from the dead? Abraham only knew he could trust the Lord to provide in His own way. Hebrews 11:8 simply observes: *"By faith Abraham **obeyed**."*

Abraham's breakthrough of favor came just as he raised

his knife to plunge it into Isaac's heart. The angel of the Lord stopped him at the very last moment and said: *"Do not lay your hand on the lad, or do anything to him; for now I know that you fear God, since you have not withheld your son, your only son, from Me"* (Genesis 22:12).

As his knife was raised to sacrifice his son, Abraham heard something rustling in a bush near the altar. He looked around and there, held fast, was a ram caught by its horns. With unparalleled gratitude, Abraham untied his son, bound the ram, and laid it on the altar as a sacrifice to his faithful *Jehovah-Jireh*, the Lord his Provider.

Although God doesn't always let us know ahead of time how He will bless our obedience, we can be confident that He will bless us with his supernatural favor in some way.

Genesis 22:14 is the first time in the Scriptures that God revealed Himself as *Jehovah-Jireh*. Of course, He has *always* been a faithful Provider to His people, but Abraham didn't fully *recognize* this aspect of the Lord's nature until that critical moment on Mount Moriah. As Abraham displayed his willingness to give God his best, God revealed Himself as the covenant partner who would provide *HIS* best for Abraham.

What is the Lord requiring from *you* today? Will you put it on the altar and allow Him to show Himself as *Jehovah-Jireh*, your faithful Provider? As you obey the Lord and are generous with Him, He will be even *more* generous with you!

42 PRUNED FOR INCREASED FRUITFULNESS

Has God ever removed something from your life? Perhaps you lost a valuable material possession or some relationship was snatched from your life. Or maybe He instructed you to trim some hobbies or entertainment from your schedule.

Such experiences are often bewildering. It's not always easy to discern whether God is cutting things away from our life, or whether these are things stolen by the enemy (John 10:10). And if it's truly the Lord who has removed certain things from us, does that automatically mean He's angry with us or that we've lost His favor?

Jesus explains in John 15:1-5 that this may well be part of God's pruning process in our lives. Rather than being done as a matter of anger or judgment on His part, it may actually be part of His plan to show us more favor and fruitfulness than ever before:

> *I am the true vine, and My Father is the vinedresser. Every branch in Me that does not bear fruit He takes away; and every branch that bears fruit He prunes, that it may **bear more fruit**...Abide in Me, and I in you. As the branch cannot bear fruit of itself, unless it abides in the vine, neither can you, unless you abide in Me.*

> *I am the vine, you are the branches. He who abides in Me, and I in him, **bears much fruit**; for **without Me you can do nothing**.*

Because of His great love for you, your Heavenly Father will prune things from your life from time to time. Yes, this process may be painful at the moment, but you need to understand that His LOVE is what motivates the pruning. He wants you to *"bear MORE fruit"* and become a person who *"bears MUCH fruit."*

He's getting you ready for greater fruitfulness than you've ever experienced before!

You see, when you submit fully to the Master Gardener, it's all going to work out for your good in the end. You'll come to see that the things He pruned away were unnecessary and unproductive, holding you back from the life of abundant favor He intends for you.

Verse 5 ends with a crucial point about walking in the supernatural favor of God: *"Without Me you can do nothing."* This means you'll never experience God's favor through striving and struggling in your own strength. Instead, you must come to understand that your fruitfulness comes from *"Christ in you, the hope of glory"* (Colossians 1:27).

The Bible challenges us to understand the two important sides of this issue: Apart from Christ, we can accomplish nothing of lasting value. But we were never designed to live apart from a vital union with Him. Because He is now living in us through the Holy Spirit, we can boldly declare along with Paul: *"I can do ALL things through Christ who strengthens me"* (Philippians 4:13).

Take a moment right now to thank the Lord for pruning away your dead branches and then living mightily in you through His Spirit. He's getting you ready for greater fruitfulness than you've ever experienced before!

43 HIGHLY FAVORED?

Do you think your life will always be easy just because you live in God's favor? Then think again.

When the angel Gabriel was sent to a young girl named Mary, her life got a lot *harder*—certainly not easier—after his visit. Yet the angel assured her of God's great favor in her life: *"Greetings, you who are highly favored! The Lord is with you"* (Luke 1:26-28 NIV).

Before Gabriel's visit, Mary had a pretty ordinary, conventional life for a young Jewish girl. She was engaged to be married to a man of integrity who had his own carpenter shop. Life was good, and she had wonderful prospects for a happy future.

Trust God, and let Him take care of the "how" questions.

But everything was about to change. Not only was she going to give birth to a son without having sexual relations, but her baby would be called *"the Son of the Most High"* (v. 32). If you face some complicated issues today, don't despair. So did Mary, and she was *"highly favored."*

Instead of immediately recognizing the angel's visit as a sign of God's favor, *"Mary was greatly troubled"* (v. 29). Gabriel sensed her apprehension and again assured her that his mission was one of favor and blessing: *"Do not be afraid, Mary; you have found favor with God"* (v. 30).

But as the angelic message unfolded, Mary must have been even more baffled. A baby without even having sexual relations? A son who would be called *"the Son of the Most High"*? A child who would one day reign over Israel with a never-ending kingdom? Mary asked a very logical question in reply: *"How will this be?"* (v. 34)

Perhaps God has made promises to you that seem incredible too. You look at your circumstances and wonder how things will ever change. If so, remember Mary. Trust God, and let Him take care of the "HOW" questions. As Gabriel assured Mary, *"No word from God will ever fail"* (v. 37).

Although Mary initially questioned how the angel's message could possibly occur, she ultimately chose to believe and obey: *"I am the Lord's servant,"* Mary answered. *"May your word to me be fulfilled"* (v. 38).

When you receive God's favor and believe His promises, He will put a new song in your mouth, just as He did for Mary.

Are you struggling to believe some promise the Lord has given you? Then remember Mary's example. Humble yourself to become the Lord's servant, then trust Him to fulfill His promises—no matter how fantastic they may seem: *"Blessed is she who has believed that the Lord would fulfill his promises to her!"* (v. 45)

When you receive God's favor and believe His promises, He will put a new song in your mouth, just as He did for Mary as she saw God's goodness in her life:

My soul glorifies the Lord and my spirit rejoices in God my Savior, for he has been mindful of the humble state of his servant.

From now on all generations will call me blessed, for the Mighty One has done great things for me—holy is his name (vs. 46-49).

Take a few minutes to meditate on this beautiful testimony of God's favor. You may want to even write your *own* song of praise. Magnify the Lord, focusing on Him instead of on your problems. Rejoice in His goodness, and humble yourself in His presence. Thank Him that you are BLESSED because of the great things He has done for you.

44 BE CAREFUL WHERE YOU LOOK

God's favor may be right in front of you, even though you only see the unrelenting storms of life all around you. This phenomenon is more common than you might think, and we see it illustrated in the story of Peter walking on the water. The story begins as Jesus is alone, praying on the mountainside. The disciples have already set out in their boat toward the other side of the lake, and things aren't going well for them: *"The boat was already a considerable distance from land, buffeted by the waves because the wind was against it"* (Matthew 14:24 NIV).

Perhaps you find yourself in a similar situation today, buffeted by the storms of life in your health, finances, emotions, or relationships. If so, you need to see what happens next:

Shortly before dawn Jesus went out to them, walking on the lake. When the disciples saw him walking on the lake, they were terrified. "It's a ghost," they said, and cried out in fear.

But Jesus immediately said to them: "Take courage! It is I. Don't be afraid" (vs. 25-27).

There's an important principle here: Jesus came on the scene amid their storm, and He was about to do a miracle and give them a turnaround in their situation. However, they didn't immediately recognize Him. They thought it was a ghost!

In the same way, God is getting ready to intervene in YOUR

difficult situation today. Don't be afraid! Trust Him to bless you and give you His favor.

You probably know the rest of the story. Jesus encourages Peter to come to Him, and Peter boldly steps out of the boat, walking on the water. So far, so good!

When your eyes are fixed on Him, you can be at rest.

But then Peter made a terrible mistake—one that all of us have made at one time or another. Peter took His eyes off the Lord and looked at his circumstances instead:

> *When he saw the wind, he was afraid and, beginning to sink, cried out, "Lord, save me!" Immediately Jesus reached out his hand and caught him. "You of little faith," he said, "why did you doubt?" And when they climbed into the boat, the wind died down* (vs. 30-32).

What are you looking at today, my friend? The Bible instructs us to fix our eyes on Jesus, *"the Source of our faith"* (Hebrews 12:2 AMP). But too often, we get distracted by the cares and circumstances of life. Like Peter, we momentarily sink beneath the water until Jesus can rescue us and pull us up again.

Notice that *"the wind died down."* You see, the storms of life are only temporary. Jesus and His favor last forever, but your difficult circumstances are destined to pass away. When your eyes are fixed on Him, you can be at rest, no matter how hard the winds swirl around you.

45 SMILING AT THE FUTURE

When you think of the future, how do you feel? Concerned? Fearful? Anxious? Or filled with excitement and hope—confident you are living in the favor of God?

It breaks my heart to see so many Christians wringing their hands in fear over the world's economy...or wars...or terrorism—when God offers us keys to live in victory despite any outward circumstance around us!

Instead of hanging our heads in despair or waiting for a bailout from the government, we can model the amazing testimony of the faith-filled woman described in Proverbs 31:10-31:

*Strength and dignity are her clothing, and **she smiles at the future*** (v. 25).

Just as He did for this virtuous woman...

God wants to strengthen YOU, so you can SMILE at your future!

When you have the Lord's favor and make Him your dwelling place amid life's storms and shakings, you can rest confidently in His provision, *smiling* instead of *fretting!* The Scriptures promise: *"A thousand may fall at your side, and ten thousand at your right hand; but it shall not come near you"* (Psalm 91:7).

This means looking to God as your Hope and Source—not to the resources or news headlines of the world.

This Proverbs 31 woman was confident in God's provision for her future, but that didn't mean she sat idly by, waiting for a supernatural Harvest when she hadn't planted anything! We're told she had bought a field and *"plants a vineyard"* (Proverbs 31:16). And as God had blessed her, she was determined to be a blessing to others: *"She extends her hand to the poor, and she stretches out her hands to the needy"* (v. 20).

In the same way the Lord blessed this woman in Proverbs 31, He promises to bless you when you reach out to the least and the Lost (Proverbs 19:17). He will *pay you back* for every seed you've sown—giving you an abundant and overflowing harvest (Luke 6:38)!

When you have the Lord's favor and make Him your dwelling place amid life's storms and shakings, you can rest confidently in His provision.

46 THE GREAT EXCHANGE

The Cross and Resurrection of Jesus Christ were the most significant events in the history of the world, testifying of a love so great we cannot comprehend it: *"God demonstrates His own love toward us, in that while we were yet sinners, Christ died for us"* (Romans 5:8).

This amazing story of love *also* displayed God's power to redeem us and give us miraculous turnarounds! Through the Cross and Resurrection, God demonstrated His favor and offered us a Great Exchange:

- Our *sin* for His *righteousness* (2 Corinthians 5:21)
- Our *sickness* for His *health* (1 Peter 2:24)
- Our *poverty* for His *abundance* (John 10:10, 2 Corinthians 8:9)
- Our sentence of *death* for His eternal *life* (Romans 6:23)

The resurrection power of Christ not only can impact your eternal destiny, but it also can bring about amazing breakthroughs in your life today. Because Jesus has risen from the dead, you too can *"walk in newness of life"* (Romans 6:4).

What needs do you have in your life today? The apostle Paul describes a time when he and his team were *"burdened excessively, beyond our strength, so that we despaired even of life."* But his turnaround came when he realized that instead of trusting in his own strength, he could rely upon *"God who raises the dead"* (2 Corinthians 1:8-9). That same resurrection power is available to you today:

> *The Spirit of Him who raised Jesus from the dead dwells in YOU* (Romans 8:11).

Because of this resurrection power in your life, *"He who is in you is greater than he who is in the world"* (1 John 4:4). The devil no longer has the power to bully you! You can overcome him by the power of the Holy Spirit and the mighty name of Jesus!

Satan has no right to steal your health, finances, peace of mind, or standing with God. Nor does he have any right to your children, grandchildren, and loved ones. You can take dominion over the enemy in Jesus' name, and he must flee from you (James 4:7).

Satan has no right to steal your health, finances, peace of mind, or standing with God.

Friend, because of the Great Exchange won by Jesus for you, every area of your life can be transformed. What a joy to walk in God's favor instead of His judgment!

47 NO NEED WAITING FOR AN ANGEL

At the Pool of Bethesda *"lay a great multitude of sick people, blind, lame, paralyzed, waiting for the moving of the water"* (John 5:3). Each of these sick people was desperate for a miracle, and they were waiting for God to send an angel to make it happen: *"An angel went down at a certain time into the pool and stirred up the water; then whoever stepped in first, after the stirring of the water, was made well of whatever disease he had"* (v. 4).

Although it may seem odd to sit around waiting for an angel to come and bring your miracle, I find that many people today are waiting for *something* before they can experience their turnaround. Some are waiting for their doctors to perform a medical procedure. Others are waiting for a new job or hoping for their boss to give them a promotion and a raise. And some are waiting for the perfect partner to come on the scene to end their loneliness and make them happy.

> *God's favor doesn't mean you can just sit on the sidelines and make excuses.*

If *YOU* are waiting for something today, I hope you'll stay with me for the rest of this important story…

The scene at the Pool of Bethesda shifts to a focus on one particular man who is awaiting his healing:

NO NEED WAITING FOR AN ANGEL

Now a certain man was there who had an infirmity thirty-eight years. When Jesus saw him lying there, and knew that he already had been in that condition a long time, He said to him, "Do you want to be made well?" (v. 5-6)

Jesus had some nerve in asking this question, didn't He? After all, the man was obviously physically impaired, and Jesus knew he had been that way a long time—38 years to be exact. He was lying among a multitude of people who were seeking a healing, so wasn't it *clear* that he wanted to be made well?

There's a point here that you need to understand. Sometimes we claim to want a miracle, but we're not really willing to *believe* God and *take action* on His promises. We're hanging around the waters of God's supernatural power, yet never actually jumping in.

However, this man assured Jesus that he had a perfectly good excuse for not getting into the water: *"Sir, I have no man to put me into the pool when the water is stirred up; but while I am coming, another steps down before me"* (v. 7).

Go ahead and jump into the miracle waters purchased for you by Jesus' Cross and Resurrection.

Perhaps *you* have some excuses for your inaction too. But be clear on this: God's favor doesn't mean you can just sit on the sidelines and make excuses. *Steps of faith* will be necessary to release His favor in your life.

Jesus then told the man to do something that was impossible for him to do! *"Rise, take up your bed and walk,"* the Lord commanded (v. 8). To everyone's amazement, *"the man was made well, took up his bed, and walked"* (v. 9).

Friend, you don't have to wait for an angel to come and bring your miracle. Jesus is already with you, and His favor is empowering you to do the impossible. You don't need to sit at the edge of the healing waters any longer. God is stirring the waters of His miracle-working power for you TODAY...opening awesome doors for you to receive His salvation, deliverance, abundance, healing, and eternal life.

So go ahead and jump into the miracle waters purchased for you by Jesus' Cross and Resurrection. God is stirring the waters so you can receive the supernatural breakthrough you need.

48 FAITH TO MOVE YOUR MOUNTAINS

I often meet people who say they want to be an overcomer—yet they fall apart when God gives them any difficult circumstances to overcome! Somewhere they got the misconception that the Christian life is supposed to be easy and trouble-free.

Yet that's not what the Bible teaches. To the contrary, Jesus told us plainly: *"In this world you will have trouble."* Thankfully, He added: *"But take heart! I have overcome the world"* (John 16:33 NIV). Yes, He gives us the power to be overcomers—but He also gives us some things to overcome! His favor offers us victory, but it doesn't mean there won't be any battles.

God gives us the power to be overcomers – but He also gives us some things to overcome!

Jesus compared the challenges of life to "mountains" standing in our way. And he gives us a startling promise about how we can move them:

> *If you have faith as a mustard seed, you will say to this mountain, "Move from here to there,' and it will move; and nothing will be impossible for you"* (Matthew 17:20).

Jesus said you can speak to the problems in your life and move them out of your way. He didn't say it would take *extraordinary* faith to do this. Even *"faith as a mustard seed"* can move away your mountains, and *"**nothing** will be impossible for you."*

Let this sink in for a moment. You don't have to remain victimized by your problems. You can go on the offensive and speak to them in faith by the authority you have as a child of God.

But I'm also intrigued that Jesus compares faith to a *"seed."* A seed is something you sow in faith, trusting that there will be a future harvest. The seed may be your money, your prayers, your time, or some other investment, but it's a key to moving your mountain.

But what should you do when your mountain *refuses* to move right away? You need to enter into God's presence and ask for His instructions…His battle strategy. As you enter His presence and put your eyes on Him, your faith gets stronger and He shows you where to sow your mustard seed of faith.

Psalm 97:5 tells us that our mountains can melt away in the presence of the Lord. In His awesome presence, sickness is healed…depression is lifted…addictions are overcome…poverty is defeated…and broken relationships are restored.

So if your mountain doesn't ***move*** when you speak to it, perhaps it will ***melt*** when you invite God's presence into your difficult circumstances. Either way, you don't have to cower in fear when a mountain stands in your way. No matter what trials and tribulations you may face, you can *"overwhelmingly conquer through Him who loved us"* (Romans 8:37 NASB).

49 A GOSPEL OF GOD'S FAVOR

Too often, preachers make it sound like the Gospel is just a matter of getting a ticket to Heaven for when we die. As awesome as eternal life will be for those who have believed the Gospel of Christ, the Bible teaches salvation is much more than that.

Look what Paul writes in Romans 1:16: *"I am not ashamed of the gospel of Christ, for it is the power of God to salvation for everyone who believes."* The Greek word used for "salvation" is *soteria,* and it is derived from another Greek word, *sozo.* This has great significance for our understanding of the Gospel.

Sozo means a lot more than just going to Heaven. It includes our total well-being: spirit, mind, body, relationships, finances, and *everything else!* It means being safe and sound, rescued from danger and destruction. Similar to the Hebrew word *shalom, sozo* often is used in the context of physical heath and emotional peace. In short, it means being restored to the favor Adam and Eve forfeited when they sinned.

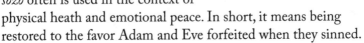

Right from the beginning of Jesus' ministry, He declared and demonstrated the all-inclusive nature of the salvation He came to bring.

When you understand the meaning of *sozo,* the Gospel preached by Jesus suddenly takes on new insights:

Jesus went about all Galilee, teaching in their synagogues, preaching the gospel of the kingdom, and healing all kinds of sickness and all kinds of disease among the people. Then His fame went throughout all Syria; and they brought to Him all sick people who were afflicted with various diseases and torments, and those who were demon-possessed, epileptics, and paralytics; and He healed them (Matthew 4:23-24).

What kind of healing or restoration do YOU need today? When Jesus preached the Gospel of the Kingdom, people got healed...blessed...set free...and restored.

Right from the beginning of Jesus' ministry, He declared and demonstrated the all-inclusive nature of the salvation He came to bring:

The Spirit of the LORD is upon me, for he has anointed me to bring Good News to the poor.

*He has sent me to proclaim that captives will be released, that the blind will see, that the oppressed will be set free, and that **the time of the LORD's favor has come*** (Luke 4:18-19 NLT).

Make no mistake about it: The Good News of the Gospel is not a matter of religiosity...doom and gloom...or endless rules. Instead, it's the power of God for salvation in all its many forms and facets. The Gospel is a meant to be a proclamation that "the time of the LORD'S favor has come."

Are *you* preaching—and living—the Gospel of God's favor today? Don't settle for anything less!

50 BLESSED BY GOD'S PRESENCE

When King David attempted to bring the Ark of the Covenant to Jerusalem on a cart pulled by oxen, the results were disastrous at first. When the oxen stumbled, a man named Uzzah impulsively tried to steady the ark, and he was struck dead by the Lord for his error (2 Samuel 6:3-7).

Horrified by what had happened, David decided to postpone his plan to transport the ark to Jerusalem. Instead he brought it to the house of Obed-Edom.

It's hard to know exactly what David was thinking at this point. Perhaps he wondered if Obed-Edom and his family would be struck dead, as Uzzah had been.

God wants to bless you, your family, and all that belongs to you today. Invite more of His presence into your heart and your home.

For three months, the ark remained with Obed-Edom's family. Instead of suffering any ill effects of hosting this visible emblem of God's awesome presence, the family was blessed with extraordinary favor: *"The LORD blessed Obed-Edom and all his household"* (v. 11).

David took notice of this! He saw that *"because of the ark of God,"* the Lord blessed Obed-Edom's family *"and ALL that belongs to him"* (v. 12). With great joy, David had the ark carried to his hometown of Jerusalem and placed in a special tent he had pitched for it.

My friend, God wants to bless you, your family, and ALL that belongs to you today. Invite more of His presence into your heart and your home. Ask Him to touch every area of your life and everything that belongs to you.

In God's presence you will find His favor. He will show you *"the path of life,"* complete with *"fullness of joy"* and *"pleasures forevermore"* (Psalm 16:11).

51 A LIFE WITHOUT FEAR

In order to experience the fullness of God's favor, you need to discover the "secret place" of intimacy with Him. In Psalm 91, the psalmist describes this amazing place and some of the benefits you'll find when you learn to abide there: *"He who dwells in the secret place of the Most High shall abide under the shadow of the Almighty. I will say of the LORD, 'He is my refuge and my fortress; my God, in Him I will trust'"* (vs. 1-2).

Amid the storms of life, God wants to be your place of safety—your refuge and fortress. But this doesn't happen automatically. You must make it your lifestyle to draw near to Him each day.

The psalmist goes on to describe the snares, pestilence, disease, and destruction that may be taking place all around you, yet *"you shall not be afraid"* (v. 5). Think of what a wonderful promise this is: A life without fear! Your Heavenly Father wants that to be your experience, my friend.

When the Lord is your refuge and dwelling place, you can walk boldly and confidently through life. When you face the devil's lies, you can rebuff them, for God's *"truth shall be your shield and buckler"* (v. 4). The Lord will protect you from harm and *"give His angels charge over you, to keep you in all your ways"* (vs. 10-11).

The psalmist paints a vivid picture of living safely in God's favor even when there is trauma all around: *"A thousand may fall at your side, and ten thousand at your right hand; but it shall not come near you"* (v. 7). When we love the Lord and learn to call on His name, He promises to be with us in times of trouble, to deliver us and honor us (vs. 14-15).

> *The more you learn to abide in God's secret place, the more His favor will grow, with enormous benefits throughout your life.*

At the conclusion of this psalm, God promises the person who has entered His secret place: *"With long life I will satisfy him, and show him My salvation"* (v. 16).

This is such a beautiful ending to Psalm 91. As soon as you surrender your life to Christ as your Lord and Savior, God's favor begins in your life. The more you learn to abide in His secret place, the more this favor will grow, with enormous benefits throughout your life. And then God promises to satisfy you, not only with a *"long life"* on this earth, but also with an incredible life with Him throughout eternity.

Take a moment to thank the Lord and give Him praise for the amazing benefits of His favor. You may also want to read Psalm 91 from beginning to end, meditating on what God has promised you when you abide in the secret place. No matter what is happening all around you, you can experience God's favor and live a life without fear!

52 FAVOR TO GET UNSTUCK

Acts 3 tells the story of a lame man who used to sit and beg outside the Temple gate. He had been lame from birth, so he didn't really expect anything to change in his dismal circumstances.

I meet many Believers who are in a similar predicament today. They feel "stuck" in circumstances beyond their control. Instead of truly entering into God's destiny for their lives, they are languishing outside the gate. And sadly, they're still looking to other people as their source rather than trusting God as the One who will intervene in their situation and meet their need.

But the story of the lame man has a happy ending, and this can be true in your life as well. No matter how long you've been stuck and frustrated in some area of your life, God can give you a turnaround through His love and power.

It seemed like a very ordinary day for the lame man—just as it may seem in your life as well. All the lame man could hope for that day was a handout, but God's plan was to give him a hand UP instead. The man must have been shocked when Peter told him, *"In the name of Jesus Christ of Nazareth, **RISE UP and walk!**"* (v. 6)

Peter then *"took him by the right hand and **lifted him UP**, and **immediately** his feet and ankle bones received strength"* (v. 7). Years of anguish were dissolved in a single moment of God's favor!

My friend, no matter how long you've been paralyzed in some area of your life—such as your health, your finances, or your relationships—God wants to lift you up today. Though you may have grown used to a life of sadness and regret, all that can change in a moment of time. Notice that it didn't take years for the lame man to recover: God changed his life *"immediately"!*

Notice too that the Lord wants to transform us from seeing ourselves as beggars. Instead, He wants to us to realize our birthright as His precious sons and daughters, entitled to live in His favor and abundance.

When God's supernatural favor breaks through in our lives, we go from sitting aimlessly to *"walking, leaping, and praising God"* (v. 8). And instead of remaining outside the gates of God's purposes, we'll finally enter in: *"[He] stood and walked and entered the temple with them."*

This can be YOUR day to enter into a new dimension of God's love and favor. You don't need to remain on the outside looking in. It's time to come boldly to His throne room and claim His promises.

But I also want you to see that God doesn't intend for this new breakthrough of favor to impact you alone. He blesses you to make you a blessing to others, and the miracles in your life are meant to be a testimony that He also wants to do miracles in the lives of those around you.

Just as happened with the stunned people who witnessed the healing of the lame man in Acts 3, those around you will be *"filled with wonder and amazement"* (v. 10) when they see God's favor unleashed in your life. They'll be filled with hope that what He has done for you, He can do for them as well.

53 SEEING GOD AS HE IS

When we go through hard times, it's sometimes tempting to get angry and bitter toward God. The enemy wants to use our difficult circumstances to cause us to blame the Lord and lose sight of His love for us. At such times, we need to hold on even tighter to the promises of God's Word. We also need to make sure we are seeing God correctly, not allowing our circumstances to warp our perspective of Him.

The Bible declares that God is our loving Heavenly Father, and He wants to meet our needs and shower us with blessings. Even though we may go through trials along the way, no situation in our health, finances, or relationships is too difficult for Him to remedy (Jeremiah 32:27).

The older I get the more convinced I become that our view of God will have huge implications for whether or not we experience the fullness of His favor. This might seem like a fairly simple thing, but it isn't. People often see God as a reflection of their flawed earthly fathers, and they consequently judge Him as cruel...perfectionistic...stingy...heartless...detached—traits that are completely foreign to our Father in Heaven.

Early in Jesus' ministry, He took time to set the record straight on this. He realized that it was crucial for His disciples to see their Heavenly Father accurately:

Ask, and it will be given to you; seek, and you will find;

knock, *and it will be opened to you…Or what man is there among you who, if his son asks for bread, will give him a stone? Or if he asks for a fish, will he give him a serpent? If you then, being evil, know how to give good gifts to your children, how much more will your Father who is in heaven give* ***good things*** *to those who* ***ask Him*** (Matthew 7:7-11).

If you see your Heavenly Father as He really is, your faith will grow by leaps and bounds!

If you see your Heavenly Father as He really is, your faith will grow by leaps and bounds! You'll delight in coming to Him to share your needs: asking…seeking…knocking. You'll understand His heart to *"give **good things** to those who **ask Him!**"*

Sadly, many people have earthly dads who aren't so kind and approachable. Some dads even *punish* their children for asking, seeking, or knocking, and this often clouds people's view of God.

I want you to take a few moments right now to stop and think about the amazing love and favor your Heavenly Father has for you. You may need to repent and ask His forgiveness if you've hung on to misconceptions about Him in the past. Ask the Lord to give you a new awareness of who He is, unimpeded by the devil's twisted lies.

My prayer is that you will gain a new appreciation of your Heavenly Father. May you come to know Him more intimately as the Father who loves you…the One who beckons you to draw near…the Provider who wants to hear and answer the requests of your heart. Let me encourage you today with the words of Jesus: *Ask, Seek, and Knock!*

54 KEYS TO THE BLESSED LIFE

Do you want to be more blessed by God? Of course you do. And Psalm 1 lays an important foundation for how we can walk in more of God's favor and abundance.

Notice that the very first word in this psalm is "Blessed." Not only does your Heavenly Father want to bless you, but He also provides you with keys throughout the Bible for how to *receive* His blessings. Two of these keys are found in Psalm 1:

> *Blessed is the man*
> *Who walks not in the counsel of the ungodly,*
> *Nor stands in the path of sinners,*
> *Nor sits in the seat of the scornful;*
> *But his delight is in the law of the LORD,*
> *And in His law he meditates day and night.*
>
> *He shall be like a tree*
> *Planted by the rivers of water,*
> *That brings forth its fruit in its season,*
> *whose leaf also shall not wither;*
> *And whatever he does shall prosper* (Psalm 1:1-3).

The first key to this life of blessing is to be careful who you spend time with and listen to. You need to make a conscious decision not to walk in the counsel of the ungodly...stand in the path of sinners...or sit in the seat of the scornful. Proverbs 13:20 (NIV) provides both a promise and a warning about our choice of who our closest friends are: *"Walk with the wise and become wise, for a companion of fools suffers harm."*

The second key for a life of great blessings is to delight in the law of the Lord, *"and in His law he meditates day and night"* (v. 2). This is similar to the secret of success God revealed to Joshua: *"This Book of the Law shall not depart from your mouth, but you shall meditate in it day and night, that you may observe to do according to all that is written in it. For then you will make your way prosperous, and then you will have good success"* (Joshua 1:8).

The psalmist paints a beautiful picture of the life of favor you can have if you obey the Lord and implement these two keys. You will be like a fruitful tree planted by rivers of water. No matter what the conditions may be around you, God will enable you to thrive, and your leaves will not wither.

No matter what the conditions may be around you, God will enable you to thrive, and your leaves will not wither.

Verse 3 ends with an incredible statement about the abundant life God intends for you: *"Whatever he does shall prosper."* Think about this for a moment. *Whatever* God calls you to do in life can prosper. Your career, your health, your finances, your family, your ministry, your creativity—and any other area of your life—ALL of these can prosper when you walk in God's favor!

So go ahead and surround yourself with people who are wise and godly. Delight yourself in the Lord and His Word. Then watch Him bring you a new dimension of favor and fruitfulness.

55 BREAKING OUT OF EMOTIONAL PRISON

When I meet people who are tormented by their past, I often find there's a forgiveness issue at the root of their problems. Although they may blame the devil or other people for their distress, in many ways they've become their own jailer. The key to get out of their emotional prison is in their own hand, yet they are unwilling to let go of their offense so they can be set free.

In Matthew 18:21-35, Jesus tells a powerful story about how unforgiveness can hinder God's favor in our lives. The story involves a king who was owed a huge amount by one of his servants. Originally, the king planned to sell the man and his family into slavery in order to repay the debt.

But the servant fell to his knees and begged the king to be patient with him. The king then had mercy on his servant and completely canceled the debt.

However, the forgiven servant went out and found one of his fellow servants who owed him a much smaller amount. He demanded the other servant to pay him, and he refused to forgive the other servant's debt. In fact, he had his fellow servant thrown into prison.

Perhaps you know how this story ends. The king is outraged by this turn of events and says to the first man: "You wicked servant," he said, *"I canceled all that debt of yours because you begged me to. Shouldn't you have had mercy on your fellow servant just as I had on you?"* (vs. 32-33 NIV) In anger, his master handed him over to the jailers to be tortured, until he could pay back all he owed.

Jesus concludes the story in verse 35: *"This is how my heavenly Father will treat each of you unless you forgive your brother or sister from your heart."*

What a sad story this is! The first servant was forgiven a huge debt, just as the Lord has forgiven each of us. But he refused to be merciful and forgive his fellow servant. As a result, Jesus says, the man was given over to jailers to be tortured!

There will never be a better time to get out of the prison of unforgiveness than now!

This story shows how important it is for us to forgive others, just as God has forgiven us. When we do that, we will live in God's favor and His blessings. But when we refuse to forgive, we set ourselves up to be tormented and put in spiritual and emotional prison. Our unforgiveness isn't hurting the other person nearly as much as it is hurting our own life.

Pause for a moment and ask the Lord to show you if there is still someone you need to forgive. Don't wait for a feeling before you forgive them. And don't wait until you think they are "worthy" of your forgiveness.

Instead, make a *decision* to let go of your offense without further delay. This exactly how your Heavenly Father demonstrated His love for YOU: *"God demonstrates His own love toward us, in that while we were still sinners, Christ died for us"* (Romans 5:8). There will never be a better time to get out of the prison of unforgiveness than now!

56 THE FAITH CONNECTION

Throughout the Scriptures, faith and favor go hand in hand. In fact, it's impossible to fully live in the favor of God without trusting Him and exercising your faith.

What is faith? The Bible says *"faith is the substance of things hoped for, the evidence of things not seen"* (Hebrews 11:1). Faith has *"substance"* and provides a confident assurance of God's unseen reality.

If faith has substance…and if it has the confident assurance of God's promises, then why doesn't it always seem to work?

My friend, faith *does* always work—but not necessarily on our timetable or according to our wishes. God IS always faithful, and He wants us to trust Him with all our heart (Proverbs 3:5), even when we don't understand His purposes.

Often the problem is that we haven't truly *exercised* our faith. He is telling us to ACT UPON our faith, but we don't believe His promises enough to obey Him. Remember…

Faith will remain lifeless, useless, and powerless until it's *exercised!*

I've heard some people say, "I don't have faith," or "I wish I had faith," or "I wish I had *more* faith." But Romans 12:3 tells us God has given every person *"the measure of faith."*

So it's not really a matter of having more or less faith. Faith is something you already have—but there's quite a difference between having something and actually using it. The Bible is full of stories about people who used their faith to see God move in their lives in miraculous ways.

Over and over again, the Bible speaks of faith:

"Your faith has made you whole" (Mark 5:34).

"According to your faith be it done unto you" (Mathew 9:29).

"Have faith in God" (Mark 11:22).

"He had the faith to be healed" (Acts 14:9).

"He did not waver in unbelief but grew strong in faith" (Romans 4:20).

"I live by the faith of the Son of God" (Galatians 2:20).

And these verses are just a small sample!

Our faith should not rest on the wisdom of men but in the power of God (1 Corinthians 2:5). It's not about what we know—in fact, it's not about us at all. It's about God's power and what He can do…if we release our faith.

And we must be clear about another factor: Sometimes we have to wait for our miracle. Hebrews 6:12 tells us God's promises are inherited through *"faith and PATIENCE."*

Just as a farmer must patiently sow seeds for a future harvest, we must refuse to give up if we have to wait awhile before we reap: *"Let's not get tired of doing what is good. At just the right time we will reap a harvest of blessing if we don't give up"* (Galatians 6:9 NLT). Notice the last line: *"We WILL reap a harvest of blessing,"* but then the writer adds, *"…if we don't give up."*

Don't give up, my friend! Your harvest is coming. Continue to believe that God will do what He says He will do!

Perhaps you know someone who seems to "have it all." They are intelligent, healthy, and financially prosperous. They have a good family and a prestigious job. Everything seems to go their way, and people hold them in high esteem.

Could even a person like this need a new beginning? Yes, indeed! Maybe they feel no need for God right now, but sooner or later *everyone* faces a troubling situation that they can't solve in their own strength. The time will come when even a person with worldly success will need something that only God can give.

The time will come when even a person with worldly success will need something that only God can give.

Naaman was such a man. As the commander of the Syrian army, he had great power and influence. He even was a person of good character, being described as *"a great and honorable man"* and *"a mighty man of valor"* (2 Kings 5:1). For years he didn't seem to have a care in the world.

Why would someone so successful need a new beginning? The answer is found in a sobering follow-up to the description of all his achievements: *"...**but** he had leprosy"* (v. 1). Despite all the things going well for Naaman, he had one terrible area of his life that he was powerless to change.

Today you may be in a position similar to Naaman. Ninety-nine things in your life may be going fine, yet there is a **"but…"**—an area of the enemy's attack that will surely destroy you if you don't find a remedy. You could easily testify, *"The Lord is blessing me,* **but…***"*

Naaman knew his leprosy would not kill him overnight, but rather it was a slow, relentless, debilitating condition that was not subject to any human cure at that time. In a similar way, you may have a problem that is slowly eating you up inside. Or perhaps, like Naaman, you have been attacked by a physical ailment that no doctor can cure.

Naaman certainly had faced problems before in his life. As a general he had successfully defeated enemy armies. But in the past he was able to solve the problems by his own strength and ingenuity. The battles he faced before had earthly enemies, and this time the cause originated in the unseen realm.

God wants to do miracles in your life today, but you need to be careful not to be presumptuous about exactly how he will bring that miracle to pass.

But now Naaman faced a problem he couldn't solve by himself. Fortunately, his wife's Jewish slave girl him to someone who knew where to find a new beginning in God: *"If only my master were with the prophet who is in Samaria! For he would heal him of his leprosy"* (v. 3). The girl was referring to Elisha the prophet.

Do you see how humbling this must have been for Naaman? He was used to giving orders, not seeking favors. Never before had Naaman been desperate enough to seek help from a prophet of God!

Naaman may have expected Elisha to greet him with the same reverence and fanfare that he was accustomed to—but it was just the opposite. When Naaman came to Elisha's door, Elisha refused to even come out and meet with him! Instead, he merely sent Naaman a message: *"Go and wash in the Jordan seven times, and your flesh shall be restored to you, and you shall be clean"* (v. 10).

Naaman was furious that the healing wasn't being offered in the way he envisioned it: *"Indeed, I said to myself, 'He will surely come out to me, and stand and call on the name of the LORD his God, and wave his hand over the place, and heal the leprosy'"* (v. 11).

Have you ever tried to tell God *how* He should do a miracle for you? Maybe you thought it would happen at the altar of your church or at a healing crusade. Or perhaps you heard someone else's testimony and assumed it would happen to you the same way.

God wants to do miracles in your life today, but you need to be careful not to be presumptuous about exactly how he will bring that miracle to pass. Instead, you need to hear His word of instruction and do whatever he tells you to do.

At first Naaman struggled to obey. He thought he knew better than God: *"Are not the Abanah and the Pharpar, the rivers of Damascus, better than all the waters of Israel? Could I not wash in them and be clean?' So he turned and went away in a rage"* (v. 12). Naaman thought he had a better idea than God did! The only problem was this: For all his reasoning and rationalizing, he still had leprosy.

Naaman's servants accurately saw the foolishness of his reaction: *"...if the prophet had told you to do something **great**, would you not have done it? How much more then, when he says to you, 'Wash,* *and be clean'?"* (v. 13)

Friend, this is exactly where so many people miss out on God's breakthroughs in their lives. They think the Lord will bless them if they do some great spiritual feat, but they discount the importance of small acts of obedience. Naaman's servants realized that although washing seven times in the Jordan seemed like a menial act, it was the key to his miracle.

What about you? Are you hoping for God to give you some breakthrough, even though you are too proud and stubborn to do the small acts of obedience that He is asking of you? Every week I receive letters from Inspiration Ministries partners who have experienced amazing breakthroughs after they were obedient to God's call to simply sow financial seeds into our ministry. The point isn't the act itself—washing in the Jordan, planting a seed, or whatever. The point is *obedience to God*, even in the little things.

Naaman finally received the new beginning he sought when his obedience was complete and he had dipped in the Jordan *seven times* (v. 14). He could have given up when the miracle didn't happen after the first few times, but he persisted.

Is *your* obedience to God like that? Make sure you don't allow discouragement to cause you to stop short. Keep pressing on in faith until you receive the breakthrough God intends for you!

58 THE SHEPHERD'S FAVOR

After years of taking care of his father's sheep, David knew a lot about the relationship of a shepherd with his sheep. Sheep that had a good shepherd were happy and well cared for, but neglected sheep were sickly and prone to find themselves in danger.

With this background, David begins his most famous psalm, *"The LORD is my shepherd; I shall not want"* (Psalm 23:1). Just as a faithful, benevolent shepherd provides for the needs of his sheep, the Lord gives provision and protection to His people as they follow Him.

As you read this psalm, recognize that it is all about the *favor of God.* Each line is a powerful statement of how the Lord wants to care for you today.

Take a brief inventory of your life, and ascertain what you need from God right now. He offers to be your Good Shepherd, giving you the abundant life Jesus also described in John 10:1-10.

Instead of barren fields, God wants to provide you with green pastures and restful waters.

Instead of barren fields, God wants to provide you with green pastures and restful waters (v. 2). When you've been battered and bruised by the traumas of life, He will restore your soul (v. 3).

When you're feeling confused and in need of direction, He offers to lead you *"in the paths of righteousness"* (v. 3).

Even when you have God's favor, you may walk through dark valleys at times. But there's no need to fear! Your faithful Shepherd walks with you, and His rod and staff will protect you from harm (v. 4).

He will even shower you with favor and honor in the presence of your enemies. No longer will you live in the land of "Never Enough" or "Barely Enough," but your cup will overflow with blessings: "More Than Enough" (v. 5).

Instead of being harassed by constant hardships, you will be able to confidently say along with David: *"Surely goodness and mercy shall follow me all the days of my life"* (v. 6). Pause a moment and read these words again. Your Good Shepherd wants you to be SURE of His favor. He wants you to be absolutely convinced that He loves you and wants to shower you with His abundant *"goodness and mercy."*

Notice that David didn't see the Lord's favor as just a one-time event. He said it was something he could count on *"all the days of my life."* Better still, the favor would last *"forever,"* even into eternity: *"I will dwell in the house of the LORD forever"* (v. 6).

Draw near to your Good Shepherd today, my friend. He wants you to walk in His favor today, and He is preparing a place for you to enjoy His favor for all eternity (John 14:2).

59 PRAISING YOUR WAY TO VICTORY

Have you ever felt *surrounded* by problems? I sure have. But the good news is that we aren't alone. Countless men and women of God through the centuries have found themselves in that very situation, only to experience a mighty victory from the Lord.

Scripture tells an amazing story about King Jehoshaphat in 2 Chronicles 20. When Jehoshaphat received word that several enemy armies banding together to attack him, his initial reaction was much the same as ours might be: *"And Jehoshaphat feared…"* (v. 3).

Thankfully, however, Jehoshaphat didn't stay in a place of fear. The passage continues by saying he *"set himself to seek the LORD, and proclaimed a fast throughout all Judah. So Judah gathered together to ask help from the LORD…"*

Friend, this is God's word to you today. You may feel surrounded…overwhelmed…hopeless. Yet you need to take this opportunity to seek the Lord through prayer and fasting. You need to acknowledge your need for His help—and He is eager to provide it.

Sometimes our prayers are more focused on our problems than on the awesome power of our God. Jehoshaphat began his great prayer by focusing squarely on the Lord's glorious power and majesty: *"O LORD God of our fathers, are You not God in heaven, and do You not rule over all the kingdoms of the nations, and in Your hand is there not power and might, so that no one is able to withstand You?"*

Today we serve the same great God as Jehoshaphat did. Our God rules over all the kingdoms of the nations. If He is for us, it doesn't matter who might be against us (Romans 8:31). Our focus needs to move from our problems to the Provider.

Jehoshaphat's prayer acknowledged his desperate need for God's intervention: *"We have no power against this great multitude that is coming against us; nor do we know what to do, but our eyes are upon You"* (v. 12).

When you are walking in His favor, you can be confident that God Himself assumes responsibility for your battles.

Perhaps you are facing a situation like this, where you realize that, in yourself, you have no power to bring a solution. You might also be able to identify with Jehoshaphat's admission that he didn't even have a clue about what should be done. However, despite his own powerlessness, Jehoshaphat knew where to look for help: *"...our eyes are upon You."*

If you are in a battle today, it is crucial to understand whose battle it really is. Though it might seem like your battle, if you are God's covenant partner I have good news for you: It's not really your battle! Look at God's wonderful message to Jehoshaphat: *"Thus says the LORD to you: 'Do not be afraid nor dismayed because of this great multitude, for **the battle is not yours, but God's**'"* (v. 15).

When you are walking in His favor, you can be confident that God Himself assumes responsibility for your battles. This means you don't have to allow anxiety to rob you of your peace, even when you're surrounded by overwhelming problems.

Instead, as Peter writes, you can *"cast all your anxiety on Him because He cares for you"* (1 Peter 5:7). Notice that Peter says the Lord wants ALL your cares cast upon Him, not just some. They are *His* battles, after all.

Jehoshaphat and his people were given the most precious promise anyone could ever receive in a spiritual battle: God promised to be with them through it all: *"Do not fear or be dismayed; tomorrow go out against them, for the LORD is with you"* (v. 17). Don't let fear paralyze you or keep you from hearing and obeying the Lord's battle strategies!

In this case, Jehoshaphat had to learn a different kind of warfare than he had been used to. Instead of focusing on the enemies, He focused on the Lord and gave Him praise: *"He appointed those who should sing to the LORD, and who should praise the beauty of holiness, as they went out before the army and were saying: 'Praise the LORD, for His mercy endures forever'"* (v. 21).

Jehoshaphat learned that praise was the key he needed to unlock His breakthrough: *"When they began to sing and to praise, the LORD set ambushes against the people of Ammon, Moab, and Mount Seir, who had come against Judah; and they were defeated"* (v. 22).

Do you want the Lord to *"set ambushes"* for the enemies that have come against you today? Then praise Him with all your heart even *before* you see the answer to your prayers!

Jehoshaphat not only used praise and worship to rout the enemies, but he and his people were gathering the spoils of victory for three days after the battle was over (v. 25). What an incredible display of God's favor!

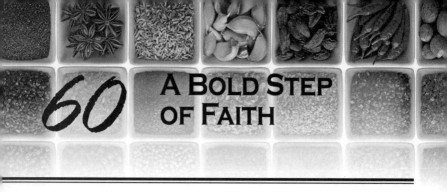

60 A BOLD STEP OF FAITH

Sometimes people take bold steps of faith out of pure desperation. After taking an honest look at their circumstances, they conclude that their very survival depends on trusting God enough to make a risky move.

This seems to be true of four leprous men who were sitting, day by day, at the city gate. There was a severe famine in the city, and it was surrounded by the Syrian army. When there seemed to be nowhere to turn for relief, the four men said to each other: *"Why are we sitting here until we die?"* (2 Kings 7:3) They understood that death was certain unless they took some kind of bold action.

These four lepers came up with a plan that seemed ludicrous. They would go and surrender to the Syrians! *"If they keep us alive, we shall live,"* the men reasoned, *"and if they kill us, we shall only die"* (v. 4).

So they got up and went to the outskirts of the enemy camp, hoping their life would be spared and that the Syrians would mercifully give them some food. But to their shock, the camp had been abandoned. God had caused the Syrians to hear *"the noise of a great army,"* and they all fled in terror (v. 6).

The lepers found the Syrian camp completely intact, complete with tents, horses, donkeys, food, clothing, and even silver and gold. At first these overjoyed men were content just to sit in one of the tents and eat and drink the provisions they found there. Then they decided to hide some of the silver, gold, and clothing.

But eventually their conscience got the best of them and they said, *"We are not doing right. This day is a day of good news...Now therefore, come, let us go and tell the king's household"* (v. 9).

This story is such a beautiful illustration of the favor God wants to give you and me today. Each of us started out in this life with spiritual "leprosy," which is a picture of sin. Our situation seemed hopeless, just like the four men in this story.

But these men took a step of faith that changed everything for them. Instead of remaining paupers, they suddenly had more provision than they ever could have imagined. Instead of living in the land of "Never Enough" or "Barely Enough," they found themselves the beneficiaries of the land of "MORE Than Enough." What a thrilling display of God's unmerited grace and favor!

Is God calling you to take a bold step of faith in order to get unstuck from some negative situation in your life?

Friend, I want you to pause for a moment to look at *your* situation today. Is God calling you to take a bold step of faith in order to get unstuck from some negative situation in your life?

As the four lepers experienced, the Lord wants to bless you beyond your wildest dreams. And then He wants you to recognize that you are living in *"a day of good news"*—news that must be shared with a lost and needy world.

61 A PARABLE OF TWO FARMERS

I once heard a story about two farmers facing hard times...

These two farmers—neighbors—looked out over their dry, dusty fields without much reason to hope. There'd been a drought the year before, and the money in the bank was nearly as dried up as the land in front of them.

But the coming year promised to be the worst yet. As another season of drought was predicted in the forecasts, both farmers turned their faces toward Heaven and asked God to send the rain.

Weeks passed. Still there was no rain. If asked, both of them would have said they had faith in God to answer their prayers.

Yet only one of the farmers *did* something. He climbed on his tractor...plowed his fields...and planted seeds.

In time, God answered the farmers' prayers and sent the rain. But only one farmer reaped a harvest. Why? Because regardless of what he saw in the natural, he believed God would bless the seeds he planted in faith. He released the seeds from his hand, and God released the harvest in His hand.

In difficult economic times like these, it can be a real challenge to faithfully sow our financial seeds into God's Kingdom. If we're afraid of not having enough, we can be tempted to hold on to whatever we have. And then when the devil comes stalking us like a roaring lion seeking to devour our health, finances, or relationships (1 Peter 5:8), we cry out to God in desperation.

To overcome the devil's attacks, we must maintain an uninterrupted cycle of "letting go" of our seeds by sowing bountifully into God's Kingdom. While the WORLD'S economic system tells us to *hoard,* GOD'S economy tells us to give.

Instead of hoarding your seeds, the Lord asks you to release back to Him what He has placed in your hands. Only then will you reap His blessings in your life and be covered by His supernatural favor, provision, and protection. He only can multiply what you sow, not what you hoard!

God only can multiply what you sow, not what you hoard!

So what kind of farmer are *you?* God wants you to walk in a loving, obedient, faith-filled relationship with Him—and then He wants to bless your finances, health, and relationships.

I encourage you to give each seed you sow a specific assignment for what you're asking the Lord to do on your behalf. Wrap your seeds with faith and expectancy, then wait patiently for your harvest. You will surely reap, so don't lose heart (Galatians 6:9).

62 FAVOR IN THE STRANGEST PLACES

Too often, people think their circumstances must be ideal before they can experience God's favor. I've had people tell me that if they just could get a new job or a promotion at work, THEN they would know they had the Lord's favor. Others have mistakenly thought everyone would suddenly like them and treat them fairly if they had enough favor from God.

We're repeatedly told that the Lord was with Joseph and gave him success in everything he did.

One of the most stunning things about the story of Joseph is that we're told He had favor, even though many things had gone horribly wrong for him. His brothers were jealous of him and threw him in a well. He was sold into slavery in Egypt, far from his father and his homeland.

However, when he was bought by Potiphar, one of Pharaoh's officials, we begin to see signs of God's favor, even though Joseph was a slave:

> *The LORD was with Joseph so that he prospered,* and he lived in the house of his Egyptian master. When his master saw that *the LORD was with him* and that *the LORD gave him success in everything he did, Joseph found favor in his eyes* and became his attendant.

> *Potiphar put him in charge of his household, and he entrusted*

to his care everything he owned. From the time he put him in charge of his household and of all that he owned, the LORD blessed the household of the Egyptian because of Joseph.

The blessing of the LORD was on everything Potiphar had, *both in the house and in the field. So Potiphar left everything he had in Joseph's care; with Joseph in charge, he did not concern himself with anything except the food he ate* (Genesis 39:2-6 NIV).

Joseph had to go through some tough times on the way to his ultimate triumph.

There is a beautiful principle here I don't want you to miss. Joseph could have pouted about what his brothers had done to him. He could have blamed God for the difficult circumstances he had gone through. But instead, he kept his heart right and experienced God's favor in the midst of it all!

In these few verses, we're repeatedly told that the Lord was with Joseph and gave him success in everything he did…Joseph found favor in his master's eyes…and God's blessing was on his master's household because of Joseph.

If you know the story, Joseph still had to go through some tough times on the way to his ultimate triumph. Potiphar's wife lied and accused him of attempted rape, and Joseph ended up in prison for several years. Yet the Lord's favor again followed him, even in prison:

*While Joseph was there **in the prison, the LORD was with him;** he showed him kindness and **granted him favor in the eyes of the prison warden.** So the warden put Joseph in charge of all those held in the prison, and he was made responsible for all that was done there. The warden paid no* *attention to anything under Joseph's care, because **the LORD was with Joseph and gave him success in whatever he did*** (Genesis 39:20-23 NIV).

Give God praise that He can give you favor and success right where you are!

Joseph eventually became Pharaoh's right-hand man, the second most powerful person in all the world. But he had learned to cultivate God's favor in his life long before that—in the strangest of places.

My friend, I want you to do something right now that may seem difficult: Give thanks to the Lord for wherever He's put you at the moment. Although He may want to set you free from your difficult circumstances, take time to FIRST ask Him to shower you with His favor even in the *midst* of your circumstances.

Thank the Lord that He is *with you,* just like He was with Joseph. Give Him praise that He can give you favor and success right where you are!

63 DISCOVERING HEAVEN'S GATEWAY

Genesis 28 tells the intriguing story of a spectacular dream Jacob had one night in a barren place, far from his home: *"He dreamed, and behold, a ladder was set up on the earth, and its top reached to heaven; and there the angels of God were ascending and descending on it"* (v. 12).

I'm sure this dream got Jacob's attention right away. But what did it mean? First of all, the ladder between Heaven and earth showed Jacob a powerful and life-changing truth:

The resources of Heaven are a lot closer than we think!

Too often, Believers view Heaven as some distant and inaccessible place, with no impact on our lives until after we die. But Jacob's dream showed him there is constant activity taking place between Heaven and earth! Because of that, amazing miracles are possible, including financial breakthroughs, physical healings, and restored relationships.

After Jacob witnessed this startling interaction between Heaven and earth, the Lord promised to give him that land and said, *"In you and in your descendants shall all the families of the earth be blessed"* (v. 14).

Jacob's encounter with the Lord impacted him so greatly that he declared the spot to be a special sanctuary of God's presence: *"Surely the LORD is in this place, and I did not know it...How awesome is this place! This is none other than the house of God, and this is the gate of heaven"* (vs. 16-17).

In the physical realm, this piece of ground was just a desolate section of desert. But Jacob dedicated it as a special place...the very gate of Heaven!

This is God's purpose for your life! He wants to bless you and make you a blessing.

My friend, this is God's purpose for your life as well! He wants to bless you and make you a blessing (Genesis 12:2) —not only for your descendants, but also to bless lost people in the nations of the world with the Gospel of Jesus Christ!

Perhaps this seems like an impossible mission, but God promises to be with you all along the way, just as He promised Jacob: *"I will not leave you until I have done what I have promised you"* (Genesis 28:15). You can count on Him to be faithful to complete the work He's started in you (Philippians 1:6)!

What was true for Jacob is also true for you today. God opens "gates of Heaven" in your life through which He can pour out His favor...provision...healing...deliverance...guidance... breakthroughs...comfort...joy—and whatever else you may need!

And once you experience the amazing resources God pours out through His Heavenly gateway, you'll want to *share* those blessings to impact others. As His love fills your heart, you will respond by sharing His hope, healing, and salvation with people nearby and around the world.

64 RELEASING KINGDOM BLESSINGS

Jesus said to ask the Father for an ever-increasing measure of His Heavenly Kingdom to be unveiled through our lives on earth: *"Your kingdom come. Your will be done on earth as it is in heaven"* (Matthew 6:10). Is there great abundance in Heaven? Absolutely! But God wants to use us to release some of that abundance to meet needs on earth.

The Bible's prosperity message is not just about your personal comfort or luxury—it's about manifesting the blessings of Heaven so we can be a blessing to others (Genesis 12:2). In Heaven there is no poverty, sickness, sin, or strife, and we should *"seek first"* that kind of Heavenly lifestyle, for ourselves and whatever circle of influence God gives us (Matthew 6:33).

Many Christians fail to see their Heavenly Father's desire to give them a portion of their Heavenly blessings in this present life—not just "in the sweet by and by." Jesus taught that those who believe in Him have *already* been given eternal life and have *"passed out of death into life"* (John 5:24). So, in many ways, eternity has already begun!

If God were truly against wealth, why would He make Heaven such an extravagant place? Instead of preparing *"many mansions"* for us to live in (John 14:2), Jesus could have constructed just one colossal high-rise apartment building with tiny individual rooms! And did He really have to show off His generosity by surrounding us with enormous pearl-laden gates, streets of gold, and an abundance of precious stones (Revelation 21:9-21)?

Whether you realize it or not, your Heavenly Father is extravagantly generous and lavish in His love for you! Paul writes that God *"lavished"* the *"riches of His grace on us"* (Ephesians 1:7-8 NASB). And John echoes:

> *How great is the love the Father has **lavished** on us, that we should be called children of God! And that is what we are!* (1 John 3:1 NIV)

Until Jesus returns, we will never experience the full measure of "Heaven on earth" that some utopian philosophers have dreamed of. Despite our prayers for God's Kingdom to be seen in our lives, we will only "know in part" before our King comes back: *"For now we see in a mirror, dimly, but then face to face"* (1 Corinthians 13:9-12).

However, many of Heaven's blessings can be experienced even in this present life. Just as some people are presently tasting a degree of "hell on earth" as they head toward hell as their eternal destination, as Christians we are supposed to experience and manifest a degree of *Heaven* on earth.

As we glorify God by walking in His ways, our lives can be *"as the days of heaven upon the earth"* (Deuteronomy 11:21 KJV). We can live as *"a colony of heaven on earth"* (Philippians 3:20 Moffatt), showing people a glimpse of what God's Heavenly Kingdom is like!

And as you read the four Gospels, notice that Jesus didn't just *talk about* the Kingdom of Heaven—He *demonstrated* it! Rather than a faraway place that is only relevant after we die, Jesus described the Heavenly Kingdom as being "at hand" (Matthew 4:17)!

- Do you need a financial breakthrough?
  The Kingdom's bounty is at hand!
- Do you need God's touch in your body?
  The healing power of the Kingdom is at hand!
- Do you need victory over an addiction or oppression from the enemy? *God's Kingdom is at hand to triumph over the powers of darkness!*

The resources of Heaven are near you today, and all you have to do is receive them by faith:

> *The righteousness of faith speaks in this way, "Do not say in your heart, 'Who will ascend into heaven?'" (that is, to bring Christ down from above) or, "'Who will descend into the abyss?'" (that is, to bring Christ up from the dead). But what does it say?* **"The word is near you, in your mouth and in your heart"** (Romans 10:6-8).

God wants to bless you through His Heavenly portals, enabling you to help fill the earth with the knowledge of His glory as the waters cover the sea (Habakkuk 2:14). Souls in eternity will be grateful the Lord blessed you with His favor and overflowing abundance!

God wants to bless you through His Heavenly portals, enabling you to help fill the earth with the knowledge of His glory.

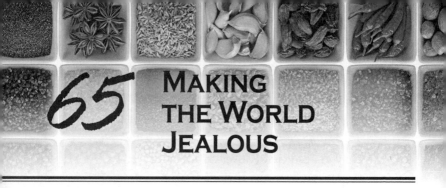

65 MAKING THE WORLD JEALOUS

When God blessed Isaac, the abundance was so fantastic that *"the Philistines envied him"* (Genesis 26:14). Paul cites the same principle in Romans 11:11, where he says God was blessing the Gentiles through the Gospel in order to make the Jews jealous enough to accept Jesus as their Messiah.

This reminds me of a scene I love in the movie "Butch Cassidy and the Sundance Kid." The townspeople asked about Butch and Sundance, "Who *are* those guys?!" You see, these two men stood out from the crowd (though not always in righteous ways!), and the surrounding bystanders couldn't help but take note.

The world should be asking a similar question when they see God's people today: "Who are those guys? How do I sign up to receive what they have?"

So even if you've never thought of God's favor as something you should pursue, remember Butch and Sundance. The world is watching. God wants to bless you in extraordinary ways, so you can make an extraordinary impact for His Kingdom.

Just as we must open our hands to the Lord, releasing our lives and possessions into His care, the Bible also instructs to open our hands to bless others. Instead of being miserly and trying to hang on to what we have, we're told to be generous, especially to the poor:

He who is kind to the poor lends to the LORD, and he will reward him for what he has done (Proverbs 19:17 NIV).

If there is among you a poor man of your brethren, within any of the gates in your land which the LORD your God is giving you, you shall not harden your heart nor shut your hand from your poor brother, but you shall open your hand wide to him and willingly lend him sufficient for his need, whatever he needs…You shall surely give to him, and your heart should not be grieved when you give to him, because **for this thing the LORD your God will bless you in all your works and in all to which you put your hand** (Deuteronomy 15:7-8, 15:10).

These are wonderful promises, aren't they? If we are attentive to the needs of the poor, God says He will bless us in all our works and in everything we put our hands to do.

God blesses us so we can be a blessing to others (Genesis 12:2). And the more we set our hearts to bless God's Kingdom and people in need, the *more* He will bless us in return.

The more you prosper, the more people will observe God's blessings and recognize what a great Heavenly Father He is.

Some Christians, displaying either ignorance or false humility, like to say, "Oh, I never ask God to bless me. That would be selfish." Yet it's even MORE selfish for God's people to remain in poverty and financial lack, because then we'll have nothing to give to others.

Mother Teresa was renowned for her simple lifestyle and ministry to the poor. But few people realize that her generosity was only possible because she raised MILLIONS of dollars each year for her humanitarian outreaches!

The psalmist, likewise, boldly declares his need for God's blessing—not just for his own sake but so that the world may be blessed through his life:

> *God be merciful to us and* **bless us,**
> *And cause His face to shine upon us, Selah*
> **That Your way may be known on earth,**
> **Your salvation among all nations…**
> *God shall* **bless us,**
> **And all the ends of the earth shall fear Him**
> (Psalm 67:1-2, 67:7).

The psalmist knew that salvation could only go out to the ends of the earth if God first blessed His people. So don't be afraid to ASK God to bless you! He wants to bless you so abundantly that people all over the world are touched by your example and generosity.

You don't have to twist God's arm to receive His blessings. He's *eager* to bless you—not just financially, but also in your health, relationships, and peace of mind. He knows that the more you prosper, the more people will observe His blessings and recognize what a great Heavenly Father He is.

66 GIVE HIM WHAT BELONGS TO HIM

I love the story about a man who took his young daughter to her first baseball game. Although she wasn't particularly interested in the game, she *loved* Skittles and was thrilled when a vendor approached their aisle.

The father gladly bought her some Skittles and then asked if she would share some with him. However, the little girl refused, saying, "No, Daddy, they're MINE!"

The girl's dad had purchased the Skittles in the first place, but now she claimed exclusive ownership over them. The father wasn't asking for much, but he expected his daughter to honor their relationship and acknowledge that he was the source of everything she had.

How sad that many of us Believers act in the same way toward our Heavenly Father. It pains us to give tithes and offerings, even though we would have *nothing at all* without God's blessing.

The Bible repeatedly declares that God is the ultimate source of everything we have:

Every good thing given and every perfect gift is from above, coming down from the Father of lights (James 1:17).

You shall remember the LORD your God, for it is He who is giving you power to make wealth, that He may confirm His covenant which He swore to your fathers, as it is this day (Deuteronomy 8:18).

Verses like these are a great reminder that none of us is truly a "self-made" person, nor can we claim credit for any financial success we've achieved. Our material blessings have come *"from above,"* from our Heavenly Father. He has given us *"power to make wealth,"* for which we should be extremely grateful.

Because our blessings all have come from the Lord, He should get the glory for every good thing that appears in our lives. And in the end, everything goes *back* to Him:

> *Because our blessings all have come from the Lord, He should get the glory for every good thing that appears in our lives.*

From Him and **through Him** and **to Him** are **all** things. To Him be the **glory** *forever* (Romans 11:36).

In light of such verses, isn't it silly for God's children to complain when a preacher encourages us to sow tithes and offerings into the Kingdom? I can hear it now: "Edith, I can't believe they're trying to get our money again!"

Somehow it has never dawned on some of us that it's not "our" money at all! Let me say it again: *Everything* comes from God and ultimately belongs to Him.

> *The earth is the **LORD'S**, and **all** it contains, the world, and those who dwell in it* (Psalm 24:1).

> **Yours**, *O LORD, is the greatness and the power and the glory and the victory and the majesty, indeed **everything** that is in the heavens and the earth; **Yours** is the dominion, O LORD, and You exalt Yourself as head over all*

(1 Chronicles 29:11).

I encourage you to take a few minutes and do this important little exercise:

- *First, look at your hands and clench them, making two fists.* This is the posture of those of us who hoard our blessings. However, there's a problem with this picture: If our hands are clenched to hold on to what we have, our hands won't be in a position to receive anything more. Even worse, we're likely to *squash* the things we hang on to if we squeeze them too tightly.

- *Now, unclench your fists, and hold your hands with palms facing upward.* You're no longer hanging on to anything, which may make you feel insecure or vulnerable at first. But realize this: When you open up your hands and release all you have to God, your hands are now in a position to receive back from Him an abundance of blessings—"More Than Enough"!

67 THE VOICE FROM HEAVEN

Throughout your life, you've received input from other people about your identity and competence. While some of their feedback has been positive, at other times people may have criticized you, spoken harshly, or showered you with negativity. You're not alone—it happens to all of us from time to time.

In the grand scheme of things, there's really only ONE evaluation that really matters. We will stand before the Lord in eternity, hopefully to receive His wonderful words of affirmation: *"Well done, good and faithful servant"* (Matthew 25:21).

But what about NOW? How can we see ourselves correctly in this present life?

When Jesus was baptized in the Jordan River by John the Baptist, something amazing happened as He was coming up out of the water:

> *Behold, the heavens were opened to Him, and He saw the*
> *Spirit of God descending like a dove and alighting upon*
> *Him. And suddenly a voice came from heaven, saying,*
> *"This is My beloved Son, in whom I am well pleased"*
> (Matthew 3:16-17).

In a concise but powerful way, the Father affirmed Jesus' true identity and His profound pleasure in Jesus as His beloved Son. Notice that Jesus hadn't begun His public ministry at the point.

There's no record of Him healing the sick, casting out demons, or feeding the multitudes.

Yet the Father was pleased with Him—and He wanted Jesus to *know about* that pleasure.

My friend, you and I need to hear this same voice from Heaven today. It probably won't be an audible voice, but it will be real to us nevertheless. Our Father wants to open the Heavens to us…to send His Holy Spirit to empower us…and to assure us of His love and favor.

When we're confident of this kind of divine favor, it won't matter nearly as much what other people may think of us. When we hear our Heavenly Father's voice, the other voices will fade into the background.

And in case you're still wondering whether God loves you like He loved His Son Jesus that day by the Jordan River, remember this: When you were born again, you became a new creation in Christ (2 Corinthians 5:17). When the Father looks at you, He sees you covered by Jesus' blood, forever cleansed and forgiven. Because of our position in Christ, we can boldly stand in the Father's presence, knowing we are *"the righteousness of God"* (2 Corinthians 5:21).

If you are still struggling with a negative self-image because of people's negative messages to you in the past, it's time for your mind to be renewed by what God says about you in His Word (Romans 12:2). No matter what you may have thought about yourself in the past, you need to meditate on this amazing fact: *"He made us accepted in the Beloved"* (Ephesians 1:6). If you're a Christian, that means YOU, my friend!

68 POWER IN PRAISE

How would you like to start an earthquake of blessings? I don't mean an earthquake that just shakes the ground and causes the physical realm to tremble, but rather an earthquake that shakes the *spiritual* realm—demolishing any satanic strongholds that are hindering God's blessings in your finances, health, or family.

Paul and Silas touched off a physical earthquake in a Philippian jail in Acts 16:22-34, but it also resulted in a profound spiritual impact. As they gave thanks and worshiped the Lord, *"there was a great earthquake"* that shook the prison and set the inmates free from their chains (v. 26).

Throughout the Bible, we see examples of God's people using thanksgiving and praise as powerful keys to overcome the enemy.

Even though Paul and Silas had been brutally beaten and mistreated, they prayed...gave thanks...and sang God's praises. And the Lord responded with an earthquake that totally transformed their circumstances!

Throughout the Bible, we see examples of God's people using *thanksgiving* and *praise* as powerful keys to overcome the enemy. In the face of seemingly impossible circumstances, God stepped in to answer His people's prayers and bring them overwhelming victory when they gave Him thanks.

Although it's fairly easy to thank the Lord *after* we've already received the victory, these stories teach an entirely different lesson:

We must give God praise and thanksgiving *before* we see the actual victory!

Just as God broke the chains of bondage in that jail in Philippi, He wants to break your chains today. As you draw near and worship Him with a thankful heart, you can be released from…

- Poverty or debt
- Sickness or depression
- Loneliness or hopelessness
- Addiction or family strife
- *And so much more!*

But perhaps your need today is not liberty from some kind of enemy stronghold. Maybe you need an **open door** of some kind—in a relationship, career, or ministry. If so, I have good news for you…

As Paul and Silas passionately gave thanks to the Lord, *"all the doors were opened"* (v. 26)!

Regardless of your situation, take a minute right now to thank the Lord. Thank Him for the victory you need…for the doors you need opened…for the answers to the prayers you've been praying. *Thank Him!*

You may have waited for a long time, but your breakthrough can be closer than you think. Even when it seems like your *"midnight"* hour has come (v. 25), God can send you a mighty earthquake of blessings and favor when you give Him praise!

69 FACING YOUR GIANTS

The Bible is a book about destiny—the great plan God has for each of our lives. Just as He offered a Promised Land to the Israelites, He has a wonderful inheritance for us as well. This is described as *"an exceedingly good land…a land which flows with milk and honey"* (Numbers 14:7-8).

But we must remember that Satan is intent on fighting us every inch of the way as we pursue the Lord's destiny for our lives. Just as God has a plan for our lives, so does the devil: *"The thief comes only to steal and kill and destroy; I came that they may have life, and have it abundantly"* (John 10:10).

This means there's a battle for your inheritance! Entering and possessing your "Promised Land" means you must be willing to engage the enemy.

Before the Israelites actually entered the Promised Land, God had already given it to them! They were the rightful owners, because God had given the land to Abraham and his descendants (Genesis 12:7). And after Moses led the Israelites to the edge of the Promised Land, Joshua was told to lead them into this wonderful inheritance.

Yet there was a problem. When they got to the Promised Land, it was occupied by powerful nations that had lived there a long time. Even though the land belonged to the Israelites, they faced inevitable war as they crossed the Jordan to take possession of it. But Joshua refused to back down in fear. He knew the covenant promises made to Abraham hundreds of years earlier were still in effect.

It's crucial to understand that having the *title* to our "Promised Land" is not the same thing as *occupying* or *possessing* it. The challenge for you and me is to take possession of what is rightfully ours (Joshua 21:43). We must claim our inheritance!

You must be clear on this: God's will for you is health, prosperity, peace, and hope. The devil's will is to cause you sickness, anxiety, poverty, and fear. The enemy is intent on destroying your relationship with God and with your family. He won't stop until he has killed and destroyed you spiritually, physically, financially, and in every other way possible.

> *God has given you all the tools you need to win the battle. You can overcome the enemy and experience victory!*

So which will it be: God's will or Satan's? In many ways, the choice is yours. If you're like many people, your life is somewhere in-between. You want God's will for your life, but you also see ways Satan has hindered you from full obedience and victory. You see places in your heart that you've allowed to become enemy strongholds...places you've not fully submitted to God...places where you've allowed your flesh to rule.

God has given you all the tools you need to win the battle. So if you are struggling today with your marriage, your children, your finances, your health...or if you are bound by addictive habits, fear, depression, or loneliness...you can overcome the enemy and experience victory over these circumstances in your life.

However, claiming your inheritance requires having courage

to confront the "giants" that seem to block your path and prevent you from possessing what God has already given you.

In Numbers 13, God instructs Moses to send out 12 spies to view the Promised Land before the Israelites would enter it. After 40 days, 10 of the spies return with a mixed report:

> *We went to the land where you sent us. It truly flows with milk and honey, and this is its fruit. Nevertheless the people who dwell in the land are strong; the cities are fortified and very large; moreover we saw the descendants of Anak [giants] there* (Numbers 13:27-28).

These 10 spies saw that God had given them a fantastic land of abundance, but they saw no way they could actually possess such a land, for it was inhabited by strong enemies and impregnable fortresses.

It's time to wage spiritual warfare and take back what the enemy has stolen from you.

Perhaps this sounds like your life today. You've heard about a place of victory and abundance that God has for you, but the obstacles seem too great…the enemies too intimidating… and the cost too high. If this is your mindset, you need to hear the challenge of the final two spies, Caleb and Joshua: *"Let us go up at once and take possession, for we are well able to overcome it!"* (Numbers 13:30-33)

God's people were at the very brink of the Promised Land. Yet they allowed fear and disobedience to keep them in the wilderness for *40 more years!*

How could the first 10 spies get things so wrong? They allowed fear to deter them and gave a *"bad report"* because the obstacles to their destiny seemed like *"giants."* Is that how your problems look today—enormous and overwhelming?

Instead of allowing a spirit of fear to intimidate you, you need to aggressively take the battle to the enemy. Passivity and accommodation will never work.

Jesus spoke of the need to be on the offensive in your spiritual battles: *"From the days of John the Baptist until now the kingdom of heaven suffers violence, and the violent take it by force"* (Matthew 11:12). You will never grasp your full blessings in Christ without a fight!

If you belong to Christ, your battle is the Lord's. Don't let any Goliath intimidate you and keep you back from the abundant life God wants for you. It's time to go in and possess your "Promised Land." You're the rightful owner, and it's time to wage spiritual warfare and take back what the enemy has stolen from you. The victory is yours!

70 FROM POVERTY TO PROVISION

Many people today are in a deep financial pit. Debts have piled up, and they find themselves needing a huge miracle from God. Often the situation looks hopeless, and it is hard to believe that a new beginning is possible.

Second Kings chapter four tells the amazing story of a widow who found herself in exactly this predicament. With her husband gone, it was hard to make ends meet. The situation had gotten so bad that she told the prophet Elisha, *"The creditor is coming to take my two sons to be his slaves"* (2 Kings 4:1).

At first it might be hard for us to relate to this statement. A creditor taking people into slavery? Yet that is exactly what happens when we are in debt. God warns us in Proverbs 22:7 that *"he borrower becomes the lender's slave"* While this may seem like harsh language, many of you have already experienced this terrible slavery in your own lives.

Financial slavery is not God's will for you! He has called you to be His beloved sons and daughters, and His kids aren't meant to be slaves of anyone! However, perhaps you are like so many people today, needing a financial breakthrough to end your bondage to poverty and lack.

Elisha's response to the widow's cry for help may seem puzzling at first. *"Tell me,"* he asks her, *"**what do you have** in the house?"* (v. 2) Instead of offering to give her something from his own resources, he first inquires about the resources this woman already has.

"What do you *have?!*" That is God's question to us as well. He never asks us for something we *don't* have, but He rightfully expects us to surrender everything we do have to Him. Yet how can someone who is on the verge of financial ruin be expected to surrender even the little bit that they still have? It is here that the story starts getting exciting.

The widow clearly doesn't like Elisha's question. "*Your maidservant has **nothing** in the house **but** a jar of oil,*" she replies (v. 2). While her first thought was that she had "*nothing,*" she remembered a "*but*"—a jar of oil.

Within a very short period of time, this impoverished widow went from financial ruin to a plentiful supply.

Perhaps you are in exactly that circumstance today. You feel as though you have "nothing." Yes, you do have some trivial-seeming resources, but they seem worthless in the face of the extreme financial need that you are facing.

However, Elisha saw the situation much differently: Her small jar of oil could become the "seed" to bring her prosperity she never dreamed was possible!

Then Elisha gave the widow some rather peculiar advice: "*Go, borrow vessels from everywhere, from all your neighbors—empty vessels; do not gather just a few. And when you have come in, you shall shut the door behind you and your sons; then pour it into all those vessels, and set aside the full ones*" (vs. 3-4).

Why would the widow need *empty vessels*, when she seemingly had nothing to put in them? The neighbors probably thought she was getting a little wacky at this point! She was preparing for a miracle, even when none seemed possible. Perhaps you have received this same response from people around you when you tell them your breakthrough is at hand!

Elisha went on to tell her to *"shut the door"* behind her. Friends, there is a time when we need to enter into the presence of God and shut the door behind us. We need to shut the door on the devil. We need to shut the door on our nay saying neighbors. We need to shut the door to *anything* that would keep us from our new beginning of God's favor in our life.

Note that the miracle doesn't begin until the widow starts to **pour out** what she has. If we give, the Bible says, we will receive back an abundant return (Luke 6:38). This woman learned to sacrificially sow a seed out of her lack, and this became the key to her abundant prosperity.

Within a very short period of time, this impoverished widow went from financial ruin to a plentiful supply. Not only was her debt paid off, but she and her sons also had more than enough to live on. Elisha told her, *"Go, sell the oil and pay your debt; and you and your sons live on the rest"* (v. 7). Her scarcity was reversed when she obediently poured out what she had.

Sometimes we think that our situation is so bleak that, at best, it will surely take a long time to dig out of the pit we are in. And sometimes it does. But the story of this distressed widow shows that incredible things can happen when we obey God's instructions: His favor can suddenly transform our situation from poverty to provision.

71 FEASTS THAT BRING FAVOR

In Exodus 23 and Leviticus 23, God describes amazing blessings that His people can receive when they celebrate the Feasts of Passover, Pentecost, and Tabernacles. God calls these His *"appointed times,"* when He wants to bless us with extraordinary blessings and breakthroughs like these:

1. An Angel of God will be assigned to protect you and lead you to your miracles.
2. God will be an enemy to your enemies.
3. The Lord will prosper you.
4. God will take sickness away from you.
5. You will not die before your appointed time.
6. Increase and an inheritance will be yours.
7. What the enemy has stolen will be returned to you.

These special feasts provide us with a fantastic opportunity to receive a new beginning from God. For example, in preparation for the first Passover, the Lord told Moses, *"This month shall be the beginning of months for you; it is to be the first month of the year to you"* (Exodus 12:2).

God's statement that Passover is *"the beginning of months"* and "the first month of the year" may sound surprising, since the Jewish New Year is technically celebrated on Rosh Hashanah, which is in the fall of the year. Yet Passover was such a momentous event that God wanted His people to recognize it as a time of new beginnings in their lives.

Passover was the beginning of the Israelites' deliverance from bondage in Egypt. It's also a picture of our deliverance from sin and death by Jesus' death and Resurrection, making us new creatures in Him (2 Corinthians 5:17).

At Passover each family was instructed to sacrifice an unblemished lamb (Exodus 12:3-6). This is a powerful foreshadowing of Jesus, *"the Lamb of God who takes away the sin of the world"* (John 1:29). He was the perfect sacrifice for us on the Cross, because He was *"unblemished and spotless"* (1 Peter 1:18-19) and *"without sin"* (Hebrews 4:15).

But this requirement of an unblemished Passover lamb also speaks of another crucial issue:

We must give God our *best!*

Despite these clear instructions, God later has to rebuke the priests for dishonoring Him by sacrificing blemished animals (Malachi 1:6-14). Rather than giving God unblemished sacrifices, the Israelites were presenting lambs that were blind, lame, or sick. Instead of sacrificing the best of their flocks, they were giving the Lord their surplus and their rejects!

As we celebrate Passover and the other *"appointed times"* feasts, it's a good time to search our hearts and see whether or not we are truly presenting our best to the Lord—that which is costly and valuable (1 Chronicles 21:24). Are we giving Him the *best* of our time, our talents, and our treasure? He gave His best to us, and He deserves no less than our best in return.

At the first Passover, the Israelites were instructed to put the blood of a lamb on the door posts and lintel of their houses.

This represented God's protection and provision, as the Lord told His people:

> *The blood shall be a sign for you on the houses where you live; and when I see the blood I will pass over you, and* **no plague will befall you** *to destroy you when I strike the land of Egypt* (Exodus 12:13).

Just as the Lord supernaturally intervened in the lives of His people during the first Passover, He wants to give YOU miraculous breakthroughs during these special seasons of His favor. He says, *"You shall observe this event as an ordinance for you and your children* **forever**"(Exodus 12:24).

God gave His best to us, and He deserves no less than our best in return.

Along with the Feasts of Pentecost and Tabernacles, Passover is part of a cycle of giving and receiving between God and His people…a cycle of seedtime and harvest. The children of Israel were blessed as they observed this rhythm of living in the covenant promises of God—and YOU can be blessed as well! If you will take a step of faith and obedience…if you will come before God to honor Him with your worship…if you will prepare a *special* offering…then these special feasts can provide a special time for miracles and breakthroughs in your life.

Whatever your needs are today—a physical healing…a deliverance from your enemies…a healing in your family…a financial breakthrough—as you obey the Lord and do what He asks you to do during these special seasons, get ready for God to step into the circumstances of your life and bless you!

72 FROM FAILURE TO FAVOR

The Bible makes it clear that God can forgive us and restore us after we've fallen in some way. As we acknowledge our sins and receive Jesus as our Savior, our sins are forgiven and we are now free to live our lives in God's favor!

Before his conversion, the apostle Paul was a persecutor of Christians. When he looked back on his life before Christ, he described himself as the *"foremost"* or *"chief"* of sinners (1 Timothy 1:15 NASB). However, instead of wallowing in his past sins and failures, Paul boldly declared in Romans 8:1: *"There is therefore now no condemnation to those who are in Christ Jesus."*

However, even though the Bible says we have become *"the righteousness of God"* in Christ (2 Corinthians 5:21), there is something that often gets in the way of our full restoration: *We struggle to forgive ourselves!*

Do you see how silly that is? The holy God who created the universe declares us NOT GUILTY because of the blood of His Son, but we feel as if we are still under God's condemnation!

Peter seems to have felt this same way at one point. After he denied the Lord, Peter was horrified by what he had done. His old self-reliance was gone, but now the pendulum had swung completely to the other extreme: He didn't think Jesus could ever forgive him and use him again.

In John 21 the story is told of Peter trying to return to his previous life as a fisherman. Reading between the lines, it seems he figured his days in ministry were over. Instead of moving forward in the purposes of God, he determined that the best thing to do was simply to go back.

Yet Jesus had called Peter to a higher calling than his old life as a fisherman. He was called to be a *"fisher of men"* (Matthew 4:19). In a gently and loving way, Jesus appeared to Peter in John 21 and gave him another "miracle catch" of fish (as happened earlier in Luke 5:1-11). Not only that, but Jesus also went on to re-commission him for ministry: *"Feed My sheep!"* (John 21:17)

If you have failed or fallen in some way, you need to hear Jesus' voice of forgiveness and restoration today. Can you see His desire to give you a new beginning and bless you again with His grace and favor? Do you hear His loving heartbeat to restore you to fruitful service in His Kingdom?

The ironic thing about Peter's failure is that it actually was a necessary part of his future success. Why? Because the old, arrogant, self-reliant Peter wasn't really usable by God! It wasn't until Peter was broken that he could truly understand his need for full reliance on God's grace and power.

The good news is that Jesus didn't allow Peter to stay in a place of defeat and failure. After Peter's failure, He discovered God's grace in a new way. And on the day of Pentecost he became the *"fisher of men"* that Jesus had called him to be—and 3,000 people were saved as a result (Acts 2).

Perhaps you are struggling today with a stranglehold of failure in some area of your life. If so, the story of Peter can be a powerful message to you. By God's amazing grace, a new beginning is possible. Your failures don't have to be final. Every failure can be replaced by His faithfulness and favor.

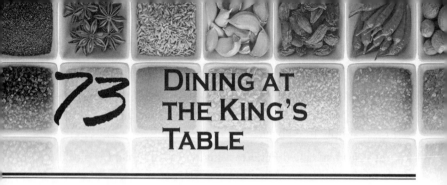

73 DINING AT THE KING'S TABLE

Jonathan had a crippled son named Mephibosheth. When the boy was five years old, his nanny picked him and fled when she heard the news of Saul and Jonathan's death at Jezreel. But in her hurry to leave the palace, Mephibosheth fell and became lame in both feet (2 Samuel 4:4 NIV).

As we'll see in a moment, this tragic beginning to Mephibosheth's story becomes a beautiful picture of redemption and restoration. The fact is that we've ALL been crippled, to one degree or another, by sin and the traumas of life. But, praise God, He doesn't want to leave us hopeless or unfulfilled.

The story of Mephibosheth resumes in 2 Samuel 9, when King David was looking for descendants of Saul and Jonathan that he could *"show kindness"* to (v. 1). One of Saul's servants told the king about Jonathan's son Mephibosheth, but it wasn't a pretty picture: In addition to being crippled in both feet, this bitter young man was living in a desolate place called Lo Debar (vs. 3-4).

David could have just ended the discussion at that point, feeling that Mephibosheth's situation was too big of a mess to remedy. But instead, David had the disabled man brought back from his squalor in Lo Debar.

Friend, I don't know your situation today. Perhaps you already have a wonderful life, with no real complaints. But perhaps you find yourself crippled in some way today, paralyzed from believing God and achieving your true potential. If so, I want you to notice what happened here: Mephibosheth was crippled in both feet, unable to bring himself back to the palace in Jerusalem. He had to be carried, which is an accurate picture of God's grace in our lives today (Ephesians 2:8-9).

Mephibosheth was understandably apprehensive about why the king had summoned him. But David reassures him, *"Don't be afraid...for I will surely show you kindness for the sake of your father Jonathan. I will restore to you all the land that belonged to your grandfather Saul, and you will always eat at my table"* (v. 7).

Mephibosheth immediately protested that he was unworthy of such favor from the king—but David insisted on showing him kindness and favor. As the chapter ends, we're told that this crippled son of Jonathan *"always ate at the king's table"* (v. 13).

God is beckoning you to dine at His table as one of His sons or daughters.

Just like Mephibosheth, YOU are called by God to be a prince or princess in the King's palace. Yes, you may have fallen, through your own fault or the failings of others. You may have felt unworthy of His favor—but He wants to give it to you anyway.

Hear the Lord's amazing invitation today. He wants to restore what you've lost. He's beckoning you to dine at His table as one of His sons or daughters.

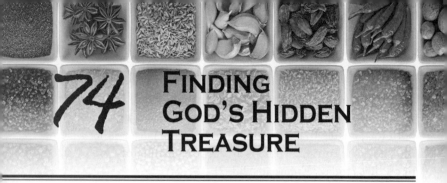

74 FINDING GOD'S HIDDEN TREASURE

Have you ever dreamed of finding buried treasure? As a child, did you ever take a shovel and try digging for treasure in your back yard or a vacant lot? Perhaps your treasure-hunting back then didn't find much of value, but I want to tell you about a treasure that is within your grasp today!

In Matthew 13:44, Jesus tells us a rather mysterious story about a man who made an amazing discovery: *"The kingdom of heaven is like treasure hidden in a field, which a man found and hid; and for joy over it he goes and sells all that he has and buys that field."*

Jesus purposefully left out a lot of the details here. Exactly what did the treasure consist of? Who hid it in the field? How long had the treasure been there, and why hadn't anyone else discovered it? How did this certain man happen to find the treasure?

Although the details are sparse, the message here—perhaps a "hidden" message in some ways—is powerful. The first clue comes in the surprising statement that the man not only bought the treasure, he bought the *whole field!* Although his objective was to obtain the treasure, he had to purchase the *field* in order to get it.

The second clue comes in this mystery comes in the statement that the man *"sells all that he has"* in order to make this purchase. Wow, you may be thinking at this point, it must be a pretty valuable treasure if the man would sacrifice all of his other possessions in order to get it! And that is an important observation, which gets you a big step closer to solving the mystery.

The third clue has to do with a central issue in the story: What *is* this "hidden treasure" that the man is so intent on possessing? On this point, Jesus tells us plainly that He is referring to *"the kingdom of heaven."* And once we understand that the treasure has something to do with God's Kingdom, the pieces of the mystery start coming into place.

The treasure is described as *"hidden"* because many people walk on "the field" of life each day and never discover the spiritual wealth that God has for them in a covenant relationship with Him. Even many Christians are missing out on the life of favor their Heavenly Father wants to give them.

If you seek God's Kingdom first, He has promised to give you everything else you need.

And notice that the treasure in this story is so incredibly valuable that a person would wisely give up *everything* to obtain it. Why? Because if you seek God's Kingdom first, He has promised to give you *everything else you need* (Matthew 6:33)! Can you see why obtaining this treasure is so valuable?

My friend, the treasure chest of God's Kingdom is filled to overflowing with His matchless favor. Don't let *anything* stop you from "selling all" to obtain it!

75 BETTER CHOICES FOR A BETTER LIFE

In Genesis 1:26, God said, *"Let Us make man in Our image, according to Our likeness."* Yet I don't believe our creation in the image of God has anything to do with our physical features. Instead, God's image means we have the power of *choice*. We must make *decisions* to obey the Lord each day.

Our Heavenly Father didn't create us to be like robots or like puppets on a string. We're not designed to worship or draw near to Him because He pulls some kind of cosmic string that makes us do so. It's a matter of our choice.

The freedom to choose is a precious gift. Throughout our life, God sets choices before us. Although He gladly reveals His will, we have the power to make our own decisions.

This means that if we love God, worship Him, praise Him, seek Him, and take time to be in His presence, it's because we've *chosen* to—not because there's some kind of mystical, unseen hand that has forced our compliance. After all, no one wants a forced relationship. A relationship only has value if it is based on *love*.

The good news is that because God created you with an ability to seek Him, you can have as close of a relationship with Him as you would like. Every day, you can experience as much of His presence as you want.

So ask yourself today, how intimate of a relationship with God would you like to have? You can experience as much or as little of God as you choose. And the more you know the Lord, the more you will experience His *favor* in your life.

Do you want to just know *about* the Lord? Are you content to just be His casual acquaintance? Or are you intent on drawing near to Him, discovering a place of true friendship and intimacy?

Your Heavenly Father longs for an intimate relationship with you. But intimate relationships take time. You can't possibly have an intimate relationship with someone you only see or talk to once a year, once a month, or even once a week. Relationships develop as a result of deliberately choosing to spend time together.

God is setting before you a life of incredible blessings, abundance, and favor. But the choice is yours.

Every day, you face a choice about your relationship with your Heavenly Father. What kind of a relationship do you want with Him? Do you hunger for ever-deepening intimacy with Him?

Today, I pray you will make a commitment to spend daily time with the Lord. Time in His Word…time in prayer…time in worship…time alone with Him. He will nourish you on "daily bread" as you bask in His presence.

Friend, God is setting before you a life of incredible blessings, abundance, and favor. But the choice is yours.

76

ACCORDING TO YOUR FAITH

Friend, as we reach the conclusion of our journey together, I want to ask you an important question: What do you need from God today? Perhaps it's a healing in your body, a breakthrough in your finances, or the restoration of your family. As you've seen throughout the pages of this book, God's favor can change *anything* and *everything* in your life. Nothing is impossible for our Lord!

But I want to close by reminding you about a few final points:

- *Be specific in what you're asking God for.* Jesus asked a profound question to Bartimaeus, the blind beggar, and He would ask you this as well: *"What do you want Me to do for you?"* (Mark 10:51) It's important for you to be clear about your request, so He can give you exactly what you need.

- *Recognize that God's promises operate on the basis of FAITH.* When Jesus healed two blind men one day, He told them, *"According to your faith let it be to you"* (Matthew 9:29). This means you will experience God's supernatural favor and breakthrough power in proportion to the level of your faith in His promises.

- *Seek and obey God's instructions.* As James 2:17 (NIV) tells us, *"Faith by itself, if it is not accompanied by action, is dead."* This means your breakthrough will come when you seek God's instructions and then do what He tells you to do. Remember what Jesus' mother told the servants at the wedding feast at Cana? *"Whatever He says to you, do it"* (John 2:5). As a result of their obedience, water was turned into wine. Those who tasted it observed that the BEST had been saved for last—just as God wants to do in your life today.

I want to pray for you in a moment, but first let me review some examples of how God's favor turned the Bible's heroes into overcomers. Be encouraged by these stories as you seek victory in your own life today:

- *If you've been victimized and mistreated, causing you physical or emotional trauma…* Remember the story in Genesis 50:18-21 regarding **Joseph**, who forgave his jealous brothers even though they had thrown him into a well and sold him into slavery.

- *If you've been ridiculed or rejected…* Remember the account in 1 Chronicles 4:9-10 regarding **Jabez**, a man who overcame a difficult childhood by crying out to God for a new beginning of God's favor and prosperity.

- *If you've suffered the grief and pain of losing a loved one…* Remember the story in Ruth 1:1-22 about how **Naomi** and **Ruth** found incredible favor and a wonderful new beginning when they moved back to Judah.

- *If you're facing insurmountable financial struggles* … Remember the story in 1 Kings 17:8-16 about how the **widow at Zarephath** found God's supernatural provision when she sacrificially provided for Elijah despite her own need.

- *If you're facing a serious illness…* Remember the account in Mark 5:25-34 about the **woman with a hemorrhage,** who suffered for 12 years before receiving a supernatural healing when she touched the hem of Jesus' garment.

- *If you've been bound by fear, depression, or some other form of oppression from the enemy…* Remember how Jesus in Mark 5:1-20 set the **Gerasene demoniac** free from Satan's bondage into glorious liberty.

- *If you've strayed from God and squandered your life in wild living and addiction…* Remember Jesus' story in Luke 15:11-32 about the **Prodigal Son,** who found a new beginning and amazing favor when he made a decision to leave the pigpen and return to his father's house.

All these people—and many, many more—received a breakthrough of God's favor when they needed it the most. They were just ordinary people who cried out to an extraordinary God.

So are you ready for your breakthrough?

Let me pray for you now:

Heavenly Father, I pray for the person reading this book who has joined me on this journey to discover more of Your supernatural favor. May You transform every area of their life as they cry out to You today. Stir their faith. Give them Your instructions. Provide them with the courage to obey You. We thank You in advance for the miracles of favor You will unleash in their life. May Your life-changing favor break through and give them the turnaround they need today, in Jesus' mighty name! Amen.

We are Here for You!

Helping to Change Your World Through Prayer

Do you need someone to pray with you about a financial need…a physical healing…an addiction…a broken relationship…or your spiritual growth with the Lord?

Our prayer ministers at the Inspiration Prayer Center are here for you. Because of God's goodness and faithfulness, His ears are attentive to the prayers made in this place (2 Chronicles 6:40).

"God does tremendous things as we pray for our Inspiration Partners over the phone. It's such a joy to see people reaching out to touch the Lord through prayer, and in return, to see God embrace them and meet their needs." – TERESA, Prayer Minister

To contact our International Prayer Center, visit **inspiration.org/prayer** or call TODAY…

United States:	United Kingdom:
+1 803-578-1800	0845 683 0584
International:	Caribbean:
+800 9982 4677	877-487-7782

Every day, Souls are being saved, miracles are taking place, and people are being impacted for God's eternal Kingdom! We continually receive amazing testimonies like these from people whose lives have been touched by our faithful prayer ministers:

Debt cancelled… *"After you prayed with me, I received the cancellation of a $23,000 medical bill. The hospital called it an act of charity, but I say it was God!"*
– MELVIN, New York

Son found… *"I had not heard from my son for five years, but I miraculously found him just two weeks after your prayer minister called!"* – Z.C., Missouri

Cancer gone… *"Thank you for standing with me in prayer and agreeing with me for my healing. The Lord has healed me of breast cancer!"* – NORMA, Michigan

Family restored… *"Thanks so much for your prayers. I've got my family back! The Lord gave me a great job, my wife was willing to take me back, and I've been clean from drugs and alcohol for almost a year. God is so good to us!"*
– L.B., Colorado

This could be YOUR day for a miracle! Let our anointed ministry staff intercede with God on your behalf, praying the Prayer of Agreement for the breakthrough you need.

Resources to Help you
RELEASE GOD'S FAVOR
in Your Life

inspiration.org/gifts

Visit **inspiration.org/gifts** or call one of the numbers below
to Sow a Seed for Souls and receive one or more of our life-changing
ministry resources to help release more of God's amazing favor in your life!

United States:	*United Kingdom:*	*International:*	*Caribbean:*
+1 803-578-1899	0845 683 0580	+800 9982 4677	877-487-7782